THE RELIGION OF THE VEDA

THE ANCIENT RELIGION OF INDIA

(FROM RIG-VEDA TO UPANISHADS)

BY

MAURICE BLOOMFIELD

AMS PRESS
NEW YORK

Reprinted from the edition of 1908, New York and London
First AMS EDITION published 1969
Manufactured in the United States of America

Library of Congress Catalogue Card Number: 70-94310

AMS PRESS, INC.
NEW YORK, N.Y. 10003

PREFACE.

THIS volume reproduces with some little ampli-
fication six lectures on the Religion of the
Veda given before various learned institutions of
America during the fall and winter of 1906–07.
The period of time and the amount of literature
embraced in the term Vedic are large; moreover any
discussion of this religion that deserves the name
must also include a glance at the prehistoric periods
which preceded the religion of the Veda. Consequently my treatment must be selective. It was
not difficult to make the selection. I have not
thought it necessary to include a complete account
of Vedic mythology and legend; nor did the details
of priestly ritual and religious folk-practices seem
to me to call for elaborate exposition at this time
and under the circumstances of a popular treatment
of Vedic religion. On the other hand, it seemed
both interesting and important to bring out as
markedly as possible the development of the religious thought of the Veda in distinction from

myth and ceremony. The reader of these pages
will, I hope, learn to his satisfaction how the religion
of the Veda rests upon a prehistoric foundation
which is largely nature myth; how it continues in
the Rig-Veda hymns as hieratic ritual worship of
polytheistic gods; how this religion grew more and
more formal and mechanical in the Yajur-Vedas and
Brāhmanas, until it was practically abandoned; how
and when arose the germs of higher religious
thought; and, finally, how the motives and principles that underlie this entire chain of mental
events landed Hindu thought, at a comparatively
early period, in the pantheistic and pessimistic religion of the Upanishads which it has never again
abandoned.

MAURICE BLOOMFIELD.

JOHNS HOPKINS UNIVERSITY,
BALTIMORE, *April*, 1907.

ANNOUNCEMENT.

THE American Lectures on the History of Religions are delivered under the auspices of the American Committee for Lectures on the History of Religions. This Committee was organised in 1892, for the purpose of instituting "popular courses in the History of Religions, somewhat after the style of the Hibbert Lectures in England, to be delivered annually by the best scholars of Europe and this country, in various cities, such as Baltimore, Boston, Brooklyn, Chicago, New York, Philadelphia, and others."

The terms of association under which the Committee exist are as follows:

1. The object of this Association shall be to provide courses of lectures on the history of religions, to be delivered in various cities.

2. The Association shall be composed of delegates from Institutions agreeing to co-operate, or from Local Boards organised where such co-operation is not possible.

3. These delegates—one from each Institution or

Local Board — shall constitute themselves a Council under the name of the "American Committee for Lectures on the History of Religions."

4. The Council shall elect out of its number a Chairman, a Secretary, and a Treasurer.

5. All matters of local detail shall be left to the Institutions or Local Boards, under whose auspices the lectures are to be delivered.

6. A course of lectures on some religion, or phase of religion, from an historical point of view, or on a subject germane to the study of religions, shall be delivered annually, or at such intervals as may be found practicable, in the different cities represented by this Association.

7. The Council (a) shall be charged with the selection of the lecturers, (b) shall have charge of the funds, (c) shall assign the time for the lectures in each city, and perform such other functions as may be necessary.

8. Polemical subjects, as well as polemics in the treatment of subjects, shall be positively excluded.

9. The lecturer shall be chosen by the Council at least ten months before the date fixed for the course of lectures.

10. The lectures shall be delivered in the various cities between the months of September and June.

11. The copyright of the lectures shall be the property of the Association.

12. One-half of the lecturer's compensation shall
be paid at the completion of the entire course
and the second half upon the publication of the
lectures.

13. The compensation to the lecturer shall be fixed
in each case by the Council.

14. The lecturer is not to deliver elsewhere any
of the lectures for which he is engaged by the
Committee, except with the sanction of the
Committee.

The Committee as now constituted is as follows:
Prof. Crawford H. Toy, Chairman, 7 Lowell St.,
Cambridge, Mass.; Rev. Dr. John P. Peters, Treas-
urer, 225 West 99th St., New York; Prof. Morris
Jastrow, Jr., Secretary, 248 South 23d St., Philadel-
phia, Pa.; Prof. Francis Brown, Union Theological
Seminary, New York; Prof. Richard Gottheil, Col-
umbia University, New York; Prof. R. F. Harper,
University of Chicago, Chicago, Ill. ; Prof. Paul
Haupt, 2511 Madison Avenue, Baltimore, Md.;
Prof. F. W. Hooper, Brooklyn Institute, Brooklyn,
N. Y.; Prof. E. W. Hopkins, New Haven, Conn.;
Prof. Edward Knox Mitchell, Hartford Theologi-
cal Seminary, Hartford, Conn.; Prof. George F.
Moore, Cambridge, Mass.; Rev. F. K. Sanders,
Boston, Mass.; Pres. F. C. Southworth, Meadville
Theological Seminary, Meadville, Pa.

The lecturers in the course of American Lectures

on the History of Religions and the titles of their
volumes are as follows:

1894–1895—Prof. T. W. Rhys-Davids, Ph. D.—
Buddhism.

1896–1897—Prof. Daniel G. Brinton, M.D., LL.D.—
Religion of Primitive Peoples.

1897–1898—Rev. Prof. T. K. Cheyne, D.D.—Jewish
Religious Life after the Exile.

1898–1899—Prof. Karl Budde, D.D.—Religion of
Israel to the Exile.

1904–1905—Prof. Georg Steindorff, Ph.D. — The
Religion of the Ancient Egyptians.

1905–1906—Prof. George William Knox, D.D., LL. D.
—The Development of Religion in Japan.

The present course of lectures, the seventh in the
series, was delivered by Professor Maurice Bloomfield,
Ph.D., LL.D., Professor of Sanskrit and Comparative
Philology at the Johns Hopkins University, and one
of the leading authorities on Vedic Literature. His
latest work, a Concordance of the Vedic hymns and
prayer formulæ, covering 1100 pages, the embodiment
of a life's study, published as Vol. 10 of the Harvard
Oriental Series, will ensure Professor Bloomfield a permanent place in the history of Vedic studies. Besides
this he has edited from the manuscripts the Vedic
ritual book, known as the Kauçika-Sutra; published
a translation of the Hymns of the Atharva-Veda, included in Professor Max Müller's Sacred Books of

the East (Oxford, 1897); written a volume on the Literature and History of the Atharva-Veda, entitled : " The Atharva-Veda and the Gopatha-Brahmana " (Strassburg, 1889) ; and edited, in collaboration with Professor Richard Garbe of Tübingen, a chromophotographic reproduction of the unique birch-bark manuscript of the Kashmirian Atharva-Veda (3 vols., Baltimore, 1901). He has also contributed to the technical journals of this country and Europe numerous papers on linguistic, mythological, and ethnological topics in general, in addition to a large number of contributions on the interpretation, textual restoration, and religion of the Veda in particular.

The lectures in this course were delivered before the Johns Hopkins University, Baltimore ; Union Theological Seminary, New York; Brooklyn Institute of Arts and Sciences, Brooklyn ; Drexel Institute, Philadelphia; Meadville Theological Seminary, Meadville ; University of Chicago, Chicago ; and Hartford Theological Seminary, Hartford.

JOHN P. PETERS,   ) *Committee*
C. H. TOY,   }   *on*
MORRIS JASTROW,) *Publication.*

January, 1908.

CONTENTS.

xi

LECTURE THE FOURTH.

THE TRANSPARENT, TRANSLUCENT, AND OPAQUE GODS—RELIGIOUS CONCEPTIONS AND RELIGIOUS FEELING IN THE VEDA.

xiv   Contents

LECTURE THE FIFTH.

THE BEGINNINGS OF HINDU THEOSOPHY.

Contents

PAGES

LECTURE THE SIXTH.

THE FINAL PHILOSOPHY OF THE VEDA.

LECTURE THE FIRST.

India the Land of Religions—The Veda.

Multiplicity of Hindu religions—Brahmanism—Buddhism—
Profound hold of religion upon the Hindu mind—Hindu
life dominated by religious institutions—The four stages
of life—The institution of caste—Caste then and now—
Symptoms of revulsion against caste—Other pernicious
religious institutions—Continuity of India's religious
history—Date of the conception of *rta*, or "cosmic
order"—Close relationship of the religions of India and
Persia—Slight connection between India and Persia
in secular history—The Parsis in India—Close relation
between Veda and Avesta—The Veda and the Indo-
European period—The Veda as a whole—The date of
the Veda—Its great uncertainty—Nature of Vedic tradition—The Çrotriyas or "Oral Traditionalists"—Uncertain character of Vedic life and institutions—Origin
of the Veda—Contents of Vedic literature as a whole
—The four Vedas—The Rig-Veda—The books of the
Rig-Veda—Theme and character of the Rig-Veda—A
hymn to Goddess Dawn—The Yajur-Veda—Character
of the *yajus*-formulas—The Sāma-Veda—Origin and
purpose of the Sāma-Veda—The Atharva-Veda—Contents of the Atharva-Veda—Religious quality of the
Atharva-Veda—Two Atharvan hymns—The Brāhmana
Texts—Some legends of the Brāhmanas—The Āranyakas, or "Forest Treatises"—The Upanishads—Literary
history of the Upanishads—The Upanishads in the
West—Critical estimate of the Upanishads.

INDIA is the land of religions in more than one sense.   It has produced out of its own resources a number of distinctive systems and sects, two of which, at least, are of world-wide interest and importance.

Brahmanism, in its manifold aspects, is to this day the religion of about 200 millions of people in India herself, a matter of interest on the face of it.   But its universal importance lies with the Brahmanical systems of religious philosophy, especially the two known respectively as Vedānta and Sānkhya. These are two religio-philosophical, or theosophical systems which essay to probe the twin riddle of the universe and human life.   They do this in so penetrating a way as to place them by the side of the most profound philosophic endeavors of other nations. The beginnings of this philosophy are found in the so-called Upanishads, a set of treatises which are part of the Veda.   The Upanishads contain the higher religion of the Veda.   The essence of higher Brahmanical religion is Upanishad religion.   The religion of the Upanishads is part of the theme of these lectures.

Buddhism started in the bosom of Brahmanism. Its radical reforms, concerning both doctrine and practical life, are directed in good part against Brahmanism.   Yet Buddhism is a religion genuinely

Hindu in its texture. It shares with Brahmanism its dominant religious ideas. Transmigration of souls, pessimism, and the all-absorbing desire to be released from an endless chain of existences, linked together by successive deaths,—these are the axioms of both Brahmanism and Buddhism. After spreading over the continent of India Buddhism crossed over into Ceylon, Farther India, and the islands of the Asiatic Archipelago. To the north it passed into and across the great Himālaya Mountains to Nepaul, Thibet, Turkestan, China, Korea, and Japan. In its various forms it is to this day one of the world's great religions. There are no absolutely reliable statistics as to the number of Buddhists upon the surface of the earth; 300 millions may be regarded as a conservative estimate of the number of people who either are Buddhists, or whose religion has been shaped by Buddhist ideas. Brahmanism and Buddhism, both Hindu products, together supply the religious needs of 500 millions of the earth's inhabitants.

In another sense India is the land of religions. Nowhere else is the texture of life so much impregnated with religious convictions and practices. At a very early time belief in the transmigration of souls (metempsychosis), whose precise origin in India is still something of a problem, planted itself

down in the Hindu mind as the basis and fundamental axiom of all speculations about the soul and
future life. This of itself is merely a theory. The
practical importance of this theory is, that it is
coupled almost from the start with a pessimistic view
of life. According to this the everlasting round
of existences is a nuisance, and release from it an
imperative necessity. It would be difficult to find
anywhere else a purely speculative notion which has
taken so firm a hold upon practical life. It pervades
the Hindu consciousness in a far more real and
intimate way than its great rival, the belief in an
eternal future life, pervades the religious thought
of the Western world.

From the beginning of India's history religious
institutions control the character and the development of its people to an extent unknown elsewhere.
Hindu life from birth to death, and even after death
in the fancied life of the Fathers, or Manes in
heaven, is religious, or sacramental throughout. It
is surrounded by institutions and practices, and
clouded by superstitions which are discarded only
by them that have worked their way to the highest
philosophical aspects of religion.

The religious life of the Brahmanical Hindu is
divided into the four stages[1] of religious disciple ; god-

---

[1] Called *āçrama*, literally, " hermitages."

fearing and sacrificing householder; contemplative forest - dweller; and wandering, world - abandoning ascetic. Such at least is the theory of their religious law. Even though practice at all times fell short of this mechanical and exacting arrangement, yet the claim is allowed that life is an essentially solitary religious pilgrimage, the goal being personal salvation. There is no provision in such a scheme for the interests of the State and the development of the race. Unintentionally, but none the less effectively, they are left out of account, leaving a corresponding blank in India's national character.

Over this hovers, like a black cloud, another institution, the system, or rather the chaos, of caste. Its grotesque inconsistencies and bitter tyranny have gone far to make the Hindu what he is. The corrosive properties of this single institution, more than anything else whatsoever, have checked the development of India into a nation. They have made possible the spectacle of a country of nearly 300 millions of inhabitants, governed by the skill of 60,000 military and 60,000 civilian foreigners.

In olden times there were four castes: the Brahman, or priestly caste; the Kshatriya, or warrior caste; the Vaiçya, or merchant and farmer caste; and the Çūdra, or servitor caste. Then came many cross-castes, the result of intermarriages between members of the four original castes. Such marriages are now strictly taboo. Gradually, differences of occupation, trade, and profession, and, to a considerable extent also, difference of geography, established themselves as the basis of caste distinction, until the number of castes became legion. At the present time there are nearly 2000 Brahman castes alone. According to an intelligent Hindu observer of our own day[1] the Sārasvata Brahmins of the Panjab alone number 469 tribes; the Kshatriyas are split up into 590; the Vaiçyas and Çūdras into even more. There is a Hindustani proverb, "eight Brahmins, nine kitchens." In the matter of food and intermarriage all castes are now completely shut off one from the other. A tailor may not, as is the custom with all other peoples, invite his neighbor, an honest shoemaker, to share his humble fare. The son of the shoemaker may not woo and wed the blooming daughter of the barber. Even a minor deviation, some new trick of trade, will at once breed a new caste. In certain parts of India fisher-folk who knit the meshes of their nets from right to left may not intermarry with them that knit from left to right. In Cuttack, the most southerly district of

[1] Rai Bahadur Lala Baij Nath, B.A., of the North-western Province Judicial Service, and Fellow of the University of Allahabad, in his very interesting little book, *Hinduism, Ancient and Modern* (Meerut, 1889), p. 9.

Bengal, there is no intercourse between potters who turn their wheels a-sitting and make small pots, and them that stand up for the manufacture of large pots. A certain class of dairymen who make butter from unboiled milk have been excluded from the caste, and cannot marry the daughters of milkmen who churn upon more orthodox principles. Even as late a census as that of 1901 reports, and in a way gives its sanction to the Cimmerian notion that the touch of the lower caste man defiles the higher:

While a Nayar can pollute a man of a higher cast only by touching him, people of the Kammalan group, including masons, blacksmiths, carpenters, and workers in leather, pollute at a distance of twenty-four feet, toddy drawers at thirty-six feet, Palayan or Cheruman cultivators at forty-eight feet; while in the case of the Paraiyan (Pariahs) who eat beef, the range of pollution is stated to be no less than sixty-four feet.[1]

Thus Hindu society is split into infinitely small divisions, each holding itself aloof from the other, each engaged in making its exclusiveness as complete as possible. Members of a lower caste cannot rise into a higher caste; the individual is restricted to such progress only as is possible within the confines of his caste. To the Pariah the door of hope

[1] Quoted from *New Ideas in India*, by the Rev. Dr. John Morrison (Edinburgh, 1906), p. 33.

is shut forever. There is little chance for national or patriotic combination.

Moreover the laws, or rather the vagaries of caste have taken largely the place of practical religion in the mind of the average Hindu who has not emancipated himself through higher philosophy. The supreme law which really concerns him in his daily life is, to eat correctly; to drink correctly; to marry correctly. The broader, more usual, dictates of religion, such as worship of the gods and ethical conduct, are not ignored, but they take a distinctly secondary place. India has at all times put the stamp of religion upon much that Europe counts as social habit, or social institution. There is not, and there seems never to have been, fixed creed in India. Hinduism has always been tolerant, liberal, latitudinarian in matters of abstract belief; tyrannous, illiberal, narrow-minded as regards such social practices as can be in any way connected with religion. Fluidity of doctrine, rigidity of practice may be regarded as the unspoken motto of Hindu religion at all times.

Fortunately there are not wanting signs of a revulsion of feeling which bids fair to sweep the entire system of caste with all its incredible foolishness off the face of the earth. The great Hindu reformer Rāja Rammohun Roy declared as early as the year

1824 that "caste divisions are as destructive of national union as of social enjoyment." The late Svāmī Vive-kānanda, the brilliant representative of Hinduism at the "Parliament of Religions," held in Chicago in con-nection with the Universal Exposition in 1893, passed the last years of his too short life (he died in 1902) in a suburb of Calcutta, doing philanthropic work, denouncing caste and the outcasting of those who had crossed the ocean, and recommending the Hindus to take to the eating of meat. The voices of other reformers are lifting. Especially the two great native religious reform associations, the Brāhma Samāj, or Theistic Association of Bengal, and the Ārya Samāj, or Vedic Association of the United Provinces and the Panjab, different as are their aims in other re-spects, are marshalled on the side of opposition to caste, as an anachronism, anomaly, and bar to social and national progress.

The dreadful institution of Suttee, or widow-burn-ing abolished in 1829, under the administration of Lord William Bentinck, by decree of government; the car of Juggernaut; the sect of the Thugs; and the practice of self-hypnosis to the point of prolonged trance or apparent death, are evidences of the frenzy-ing quality of Hindu religion, and the way it has of overshadowing individual sanity and public in-terest. There has been, and there still is, too much so-called religion in India: Brahmanical hierarchy, sacerdotalism, asceticism, caste; infinitely diversified polytheism and idolatry; cruel religious practices; and bottomless superstition. All this the higher Hindu religions, or rather religious philosophies, blow away as the wind does chaff. In their view such religiosity is mere illusion or ignorance, to save from which is their profession. But they can save only the illumined of mind. On the real life of India the great philosophies are merely a thin film. Anyhow they have not as yet penetrated down to the Hindu people, and we may question whether India's salvation will come that way, rather than through the growth of social and political intelligence which so gifted a people is sure, in the long run, to obtain.

The student of the History of Religions has good reason to think of India as the land of religions in yet another sense. Not only has India produced out of its own mental resources many important religions and theosophic systems, but it has carried on these processes continuously, uninterrupted by distracting outside influences. The Moghul conquests in Northern India introduced Mohammedanism to a limited extent, and Mohammedanism fused with Hinduism in the hybrid religion of the Sikhs. A small number of Zoroastrian Parsis, driven from Persia during the Mohammedan conquest, found

a friendly refuge for themselves and the religion
of Zarathushtra (Zoroaster) in the West of India.
Aside from that there is no record of permanent
outside influence on a larger scale, until, in the last
century, the above-mentioned Brāhma Samāj, a kind
of religious Volapük, or Esperanto, undertakes, in
the most praiseworthy spirit, upon a universal theistic platform, to blend and harmonise the best in
Hindu religious thought, with the best that may be
found in other religions.   In this way Hindu religion is more strictly native than any of the great
religions of mankind.   This is no doubt due mainly
to India's geographical isolation, and to her insular
secular history.   It has had the merit of keeping
her religious development continuous and organic.
Every important idea has a traceable past history;
every important idea is certain to develop in the
future.   We may say that a body of 3500 years
of organic religious growth lies more or less
open before the eyes of the student of India's
religions, to dissect, to study, and to philosophise
upon.

This great period of time has of late become
definite in a rather important sense.   Within recent
years there were discovered at Tel-el-Amarna, in
Upper Egypt, numerous cuneiform tablets containing letters from tributary kings of Babylonia,

Assyria, Mitani, Phœnicia, and Canaan, addressed to
certain Egyptian Pharaohs, their liege lords. These
tablets have thrown much new light upon the history
of Western Asia. There is among them a letter
written by a king of Mitani in Syria, Dushratta by
name. In this letter figure among others the names
of his brother Artashuvara and his grandfather Artatama. These names are obviously Iranian (Persian),
or " Iranoid "; with the tablets themselves they date
back to at least 1600 B. C.[1] The names Artashuvara
and Artatama open out with the syllables *arta-*,
familiar to Western students of history as part of
the numberless Persian names like Artaxerxes, Arta-
phernes, etc. This stem *arta* is identical with *arta-*
of the Western Iranian, Achemenidan inscriptions,
with *asha* of the Avesta, and with *rta* of the Veda.
The word means " cosmic order," or " order of the
universe." We shall find it later on, figuring as one
of the most important religious conceptions of the
Rig-Veda. We have here at any rate a definite
lower date for the idea; it is likely to have existed
a long time before 1600 B.C. From the point of
view of the history of religious ideas we may, in fact
we must, begin the history of Hindu religion at

[1] See the author, *American Journal of Philology*, xxv., p. 8 ;
F. Hommel in *Sitzungsberichte der Königlich Böhmischen Gesellschaft der Wissenschaften*, 1898, Number vi.

least with the history of this conception. Broad as
the ocean, and as uninterrupted in its sweep there
lies before µs a period of thousands of years of the
religious thought and practice of the most religious
people in the history of the world.

Now this brings us face to face with the tried and
true fact that the religious history of India does not
really begin at the time when the Veda, the earliest
literature, was composed, but that it begins much
earlier.   In the first place, it shares a fairly clear
common life with the ancient religion of Iran (Persia)
in a prehistoric time, the so-called Indo-Iranian or
Aryan period.[1] The reconstruction of these common religious properties is purely prehistoric.   It
partakes of the fate of all prehistoric studies; it is
not definite, but more or less hazy.   Yet, such as it
is, it counts fairly with the best that may be achieved
in this way. It is based upon the plainly evident
relationship between the Hindu Veda and the
Persian Avesta, the most ancient sacred books of
the two peoples.   No student of either religion
questions that they drew largely from a common
source, and therefore mutually illumine each other.

I am sure that the full meaning of this last statement will appear clearer after a word of explanation.
Students of profane history are accustomed to see

[1] See below page 119.

ancient Persia with her face turned westward. It is to them the Persia that conquers, or controls through her satrapies, Assyria and Babylonia, Palestine, Egypt, or parts of Asia Minor. It is to them the Persia that falls down before Greece. In the day of her greatest glory Darius I. Hystaspes carved into the Behistan rock, 300 feet above the ground, the hugh trilingual cuneiform inscription, in which he claims suzerainty over twenty-three countries. To all intents and purposes he claims the earth for his own. Among the countries mentioned are parts adjacent to the extreme north-west of India: Drangiana, Arachosia, Gandhāra, etc. Between 500–330 B.C., the rule of the Achemenidan Persian dynasty had without doubt sent out its loosely attached satrapies to the land of the Indus River. But this did not result in the permanent attachment of one country to the other. Again, the so-called Graeco-Parthian rulers, successors of Alexander the Great in the Persian countries of Parthia and Baktria, from about 200 B.C. to 200 A.D., established principalities in the north-west of India, notably the Indo-Parthian kingdoms of Taxila and Arachosia.[1] But this political relation, again, proved unstable and transient.

A small number of Parsis, after the Mohammedan

[1] See Vincent Smith, *The Indo-Parthian Dynasties*, in *Journal of the German Oriental Society*, vol. lx., p. 49 *ff*.

conquest of Persia, fled to India with their priests,
sacred fire, and the manuscripts of the Avesta, their
holy scriptures.   Their descendants, about 80,000 in
number, still adhere to their ancient religion   They
form one of the most esteemed, wealthy, and philanthropic communities on the west shores of India,
notably in the city of Bombay.   It is not of record
that they had even the faintest idea that they were
fleeing into the hospitable bosom of a people related
by blood and language, or that the Hindus who gave
them shelter knew that they were receiving their
very own kin.   As far as we know, the Aryan
Hindus at any rate, throughout their history, are
entirely unconscious of the important fact that,
across the mountains to the north-west of their
country, dwelt at all times a branch of their own
stock—the other half of the so-called Indo-Iranians
or Aryans.

And yet, the languages of the Hindu Veda and
the Persian Avesta, the respective bibles of the
two peoples, are mere dialects of the same speech.
Students regularly enter upon the study of the
Avestan language through the door of the Veda.
Entire passages of the Avesta may be turned into
good Vedic merely by applying certain regular sound
changes.   It is said sometimes that there is less difference between the Veda and the Avesta than be-

tween the Veda and the later Hindu Epic, the
Mahābhārata. This is, in my opinion, an exaggeration, but it is significant that the statement
could be made at all. The early religions and the
religious institutions of the Hindus and Persians
show, to be sure, far greater independence from one
another than their languages, but they are, nevertheless, at the root much the same. So it has come
to pass that a not at all mean part of the Vedic
Pantheon and Vedic religious ideas begin before the
Veda. Or, to put it even more paradoxically, Indian
religion begins before its arrival in India.

Yet further, beyond the common period of the
Hindus and the Persians, there is a still remoter
period which is not entirely closed to our view.
It is the common Indo-European time, the time
when the Hindus and Persians still shared their
language and home with the remaining members of the same stock, the Hellenes, Italians,
Celts, Teutons, and Slavs. In this altogether prehistoric time there also existed certain germs of
religion, and some of these germs grew into important features of the later religions of these peoples.
The religion of the Veda is indebted to this early
time to an extent that is not negligible. We shall
see later on in what way the two layers of prehistoric religious matter have contributed to and affected

the shaping of Vedic thought. For the present it will be advantageous to turn to the Vedic religion of historic times, so that there may be some basis for discriminating between what is old and what is new. And as it would not be gracious to presume too much knowledge of so remote a theme as the Veda, we must first describe briefly the documents of which consists the Veda, the most ancient literary monument of India, the most ancient literary document of the Indo-European peoples—the foundation for all time of India's religious thought.

THE VEDA

The word *veda* means literally "knowledge," that is, "sacred knowledge." It is derived from *vid*, "to know," and connected with Greek $(F)οῖδα$, Gothic *wait*, German *weiss*, English *wit*, "to know." The term Veda is used in two ways: either as the collective designation of the entire oldest sacred literature of India, or as the specific name of single books belonging to that literature. So then, on the one hand, we speak of *the* Veda as the bible of ancient India; or, on the other hand, we speak of Rig Veda, Atharva-Veda, etc., as individual books of that great collection. The number of books which, in one sense or another, are counted as Veda is a hundred or more. The Hindus

2

themselves were never very keen about canonicity;
quasi-Vedic books, or, as we should say, Pseudo-
Vedic books were composed at a very late date,
when the various and peculiar sources of early inspiration had dried up; they kept pouring new, mostly
sour wine into the old skins. The huge Concordance
of the Vedas, which it has been my fate to publish
this year (1906), absorbs about 120 texts more or
less Vedic.

It is truly humiliating to students of ancient India
to have to answer the inevitable question as to the
age of the Veda with a meek, "We don't know." As
regards their texture, the books of the Veda claim
great antiquity with no uncertain voice. One should
like to see this intrinsically archaic quality held up
by actual dates ; those same, almost fabulous, yet perfectly authentic dates that are being bandied about
in the ancient history of Assyria, Babylonia, and
Egypt.   The late Professor William D. Whitney left
behind the witty saying that Hindu dates are merely
ten-pins set up to be bowled down again. This is
not altogether so.   Buddha died 477 B.C. Alexander
invaded India in 326 B.C.   In the year 315 B.C.
Candragupta, or Sandrakottos, "Alexander-Killer,"
as Greek writers ominously mouthed over his name,
led a successful revolt against Alexander's prefects
and established the Maurya dynasty in Pātaliputra,

the Palibothra of the Greeks, the Patna of to-day.
The most important date in Hindu secular history
is that of Candragupta's grandson, the famous
Buddhist Emperor Açoka or Piyadassi, who ruled
India from north to south around about 250 B.C. His
edicts, carved into rock all over his great empire,
show us the singular spectacle of a great ruler who
used his power to propagate his religion peacefully.
His inscriptions upon pillars and rocks boast not
of victory or heroic deed; they exhort his people to
virtue, warn against sin, and plead for tolerance and
love of humanity. This is an important date in the
history of India, but an even more important date
in the history of good manners.

Unquestionably a century or two must have passed
between the conclusion of the Vedic period and the
beginnings of Buddhism. Buddhist literature presupposes Brahmanical literature and religion in a
stage of considerable advancement beyond the Vedas.
We are, therefore, reasonably safe in saying that the
real Vedic period was concluded about 700 B.C.
We are further on safe ground in demanding a number of centuries for the much stratified language,
literature, and religion of the Veda. But how many?
It is as easy to imagine three as thirteen or twenty-
three. Only one thing is certain. Vedic ideas are
very old. I have noted the fact that the concept *that*

"cosmic or universal order," is found in cut and dried
Iranian names in Western Asia as early as 1600 B.C.
I am, for my part, and I think I voice many scholars,
now much more inclined to listen to an early date,
say 2000 B.C., for the beginnings of Vedic literary
production, and to a much earlier date for the
beginnings of the institutions and religious concepts
which the Veda has derived from those prehistoric
times which cast their shadows forward into the
records that are in our hands.   Anyhow, we must
not be beguiled by that kind of conservatism which
merely salves the conscience into thinking that
there is better proof for any later date, such as
1500, 1200, or 1000 B.C., rather than the earlier
date of 2000 B.C.   Once more, frankly, we do not
know.

Vedic tradition is in some respects the most remarkable in recorded history.   From the entire
Vedic period we have not one single piece of anti-
quarian or archæological material, not one bit of real
property ; not a building, nor a monument ; not a
coin, jewel, or utensil ;—nothing but winged words.
Even the manuscripts of these precious texts,
splendid as we know their authority to be on inner
evidence are of comparatively recent date.   We do
not know when the Vedas were first committed to
writing.   Even if they were written down during the

Vedic period itself, as I think altogether likely, the early manuscripts were certain to perish in the furious Indian climate. They must, in that case, have been saved by diligent copying and recopying. The majority of the manuscripts upon which are based our editions of Vedic texts date from recent centuries. Manuscripts that date back to the fourteenth century of our era are rare ; only a very few go back to the twelfth.

Here, however, enters one of the curiosities of Hindu religious life. The adherents of a certain Veda or Vedic school, no matter whether the text of that school was reduced to writing or not, must, in theory, know their texts by heart. These are the so-called Çrotriyas or "Oral Traditionalists." They live to this day, being, as it were, living manuscripts of their respective Vedas. The eminent Hindu scholar, the late Shankar Pandurang Pandit, tells us in the preface to his great Bombay edition of the Atharva-Veda how he used three of these oral reciters of the Atharva-Veda out of a total of only four that were at that time still alive in the Dekkhan ; and how their oral authority proved to be quite as weighty as the written authority of his manuscripts. These living manuscripts were respectively, Messrs. Bāpujī Jīvanrām ; Keçava Bhat bin Dājī Bhat ; and Venkan Bhatjī, the last " the most celebrated Atharva

Vaidíka in the Dekkhan." Mr. Pandit cites them by *sigla*, quite in the manner of inanimate manuscripts, respectively, as Bp, K, and V. They are, I believe, now all dead.

We are waiting now for the time when the India Exploration Society shall step out from its existence on paper, and take hold of the shovel and the spade. With bated breath we shall then be watching to see whether great good fortune will make it possible to dig through the thick crust of centuries that are piled upon the Vedic period. If so, it will be something like the revelation of the Mycenean age that was found at the root of Hellenic civilisation. Until that time Vedic life and institutions, reported only by word of mouth, must remain an uncertain quantity. The hymns of the Veda are to a considerable degree cloudy, turgid, and mystic; taken by themselves they will never yield a clear picture of human life that fits any time or place. We have from the entire Vedic period no annals except priestly annals, or such at least as have been edited by priests. It is as though we relied upon cloister chronicles alone for our knowledge of the politics and institutions of a certain time. Or, to use an even homelier comparison, as though we had to reconstruct the social conditions of a more modern time from an intercepted boarding-school correspondence. The poets, or priestly writers of the Veda are entirely preoccupied with their own interests; if we want anything like secular records of India we must look to a later time.

We do not even know exactly what a term as familiar as *rāja* (*rēx*) "King," meant in those early days. Was a Rāja a great potentate, or merely a tribal chieftain? We know that the early Vedic period was a cattle-raising age. The lowing of kine was lovely music to the ear of the Vedic poet. But there were also workers in metals, chariots, navigation of some kind, gold, jewels, and trade. This is all too vague, and to some extent introduces uncertain quantities into our estimation of Vedic religion.

At an unknown date then, as we have had to confess reluctantly, Aryan tribes or clans (*viç* [1]) began to migrate from the Iranian highlands to the north of the Hindu-Kush Mountains into the north-west of India, the plains of the river Indus and its tributaries, the Panjab, or the land of the five streams. [2]

---

[1] From this word is derived *vaiçya*, the later name of the third, or agricultural and merchant caste.

[2] Professor E. W. Hopkins, *Journal of the American Oriental Society*, vol. xix., pp. 19–28. argues that the majority of the Vedic hymns were composed farther east than the Panjab, in the region of the modern city of Amballa, between the rivers Sarasouti and Ghuggar.

The river Ganges, so essential to a picture of India in historical times, and even more bound up with all Western poetic fancies about India, is scarcely mentioned in the Rig-Veda. This same text is full of allusions to the struggles of the fair-skinned Aryas with the dark-skinned aborigines, the Dasyus. The struggle is likely to have been bitter. The spread of Aryan civilisation was gradual, and resulted finally in the up-building of a people whose civilisation was foreign and superior, but whose race quality was determined a good deal by the overwhelmingly large, native, dark-skinned, non-Aryan population. At the beginning of our knowledge of India we are face to face with an extensive poetical literature, in set metres. This is crude on the whole, even when compared with classical Sanskrit literature of later times. Yet, it shows, along with uncouth naïveté and semi-barbarous turgidity, a good deal of beauty and elevation of thought, and a degree of skill bordering on the professional, in the handling of language and metre. That this product was not created out of nothing on Indian soil follows from the previously mentioned close connection with the earliest product of Persian literature, the Avesta.[1] Even the metric types of Veda and Avesta are closely related.

[1] See above, p. 13.

Vedic literature, in its first intention, is throughout religious, or it deals with institutions that have come under the control of religion. It includes hymns, prayers, and sacred formulas, offered by priests to the gods in behalf of rich lay sacrificers; charms for witchcraft, medicine, and other homely practices, manipulated by magicians and medicinemen, in the main for the plainer people. From a later time come expositions of the sacrifice, illustrated by legends, in the manner of the Jewish Talmud. Then speculations of the higher sort, philosophic, cosmic, psycho-physical, and theosophic, gradually growing up in connection with and out of the simpler beliefs. Finally there is a considerable body of set rules for conduct in every-day secular life, at home and abroad, that is, a distinct literature of customs and laws. This is the Veda as a whole.

The Veda consists, as we have seen, of considerably more than a hundred books, written in a variety of slightly differentiated dialects and styles. Some of the Vedic books are not yet published, or even unearthed. At the base of this entire canon, if we may so call it, lie four varieties of metrical composition, or in some cases, prayers in sacred, solemn prose. These are known as the Four Vedas in the narrower sense: the Rig-Veda, the Yajur-Veda, the Sāma-Veda, and the Atharva-Veda. These four names

come from a somewhat later Vedic time ; they do
not coincide exactly with the earlier names, nor do
they fully correspond to the contents of the texts
themselves. The earlier names refer rather to the
different styles of composition, than to canonical collections. They are *ṛcaḥ*, "stanzas of praise"; *yajūṅshi*, "liturgical stanzas and formulas"; *sāmāni*, "melodies"; and *atharvāṅgirasaḥ*, "blessings and curses."
The book which goes by the name of Rig-Veda contains not only " stanzas of praise," but—in its later
parts—also "blessings and curses,"as well as most of
the stanzas which form the text to the *sāman*-melo-
dies of the Sāma-Veda. The Atharva-Veda contains
ṛcah, "stanzas of praise," and *yajūṅshi*, "liturgical
stanzas,"mostly worked over for its own purposes, as
well as its very own " blessings and curses." The Yajur-Veda also contains materials of the other Vedic
types in addition to its main topic, the liturgy. The
Sāma-Veda is merely a collection of a certain kind
of *ṛcaḥ*, or "stanzas of praise," which are derived with
some variants and additions from the Rig-Veda, and
are here set to music which is indicated by musical
notations.

The Rig-Veda is, on the whole, the oldest as well
as the most important of the four collections. Its
language is a priestly, very high, or very literary
speech. This we may call by distinction the hieratic

language of the Veda. It is based upon a very old popular dialect, into which the poets, to serve their own needs, have introduced many new words and speech-forms. So, for instance, the great liking of the hieratic language for verbs derived from nouns, the so-called denominative or denominal verbs, surrounds the style of the Rig-Veda with an air of turgidity and stiltedness which is far from being archaic. A hieratic poet prefers to say " give battle "(*pṛtanāyati, pṛtanyati*), rather than "fight"; "cultivate the gods" (*devayati*), rather than " be pious "; "show a kind disposition" (*sumanasyate*), rather than "be friendly," etc.

A little over 1000 hymns, containing about 10,000 stanzas, equal in bulk to Homer's poems, are divided into ten *mandalas*, "circles," or, as we should say, books. Inside of these books the hymns are arranged according to a regular scheme: first, in the order of the number of hymns addressed to a particular god, beginning with the largest number and continuing in a descending scale. Next, each god's hymns are arranged according to the length of each single hymn, again in a descending scale. Six of these ten books (ii–vii), the so-called "family-books," form the nucleus of the collection. Each of these is supposed to have been composed by a different Rishi, poet or seer, or rather by some family of poets who would

fondly derive their descent from such a Rishi. The
hymns themselves state this repeatedly—such and
such a poet has seen[1] such and such a hymn—: the
exact value of this claim is not easily estimated.
The names of these traditional Rishis have a good
ring in India at all times. They are in the order of
Books ii–vii, Grtsamada, Viçvāmitra, Vāmadeva, Atri,
Bharadvāja, and Vasishtha. The eighth book and
the first fifty hymns of the first book are ascribed
to the family of Kanva; they are marked off even
superficially from the rest, because they are arranged
strophically in groups of two or three stanzas. These
form the bulk of those stanzas which, set to music,
reappear in the Sāma-Veda. The ninth book, a kind
of Bacchic collection or text-book, is addressed to
the deified plant *soma*, and the liquor pressed from
it.[2] This *soma* drink furnishes by far the most precious libation to the gods. They are supposed to
intoxicate themselves with it unto great deeds of
valor. The remainder of the first book and the
entire tenth book are more miscellaneous in character and problematic as to intention and arrangement. To some extent, though by no means entirely, they are of later origin and from a different
sphere, in part of distinctly popular character, very

[1] That is, has had revealed to him.
[2] See below, p. 145.

much like and often identical with the hymns of the Atharva-Veda.

On the whole and in the main, as we shall see, the Rig-Veda is a collection of priestly hymns addressed to the gods of the Vedic Pantheon. The chanting of these hymns is regularly accompanied by libations of the intoxicating drink called *soma*, and of melted butter, or ghee (*ghrta*). The enduring interest of the Rig-Veda as literature lies in those old priestly poets' vision of the beauty, the majesty, and the power of the gods, and in the myths and legends told of them, or, more often, merely alluded to in connection with them. But the paramount importance of the Rig-Veda is after all not as literature, but as philosophy. Its mythology represents a clearer, even if not always chronologically earlier stage of thought and religious development than is to be found in any parallel literature. On one side at least it is primitive in conception, and constructive under our very eyes : how a personal god develops by personification out of a visible fact in nature (anthropomorphosis) no literary document in the world teaches as well as the Rig-Veda. The original nature of the Vedic gods, however, is not always clear, not as clear as was once fondly thought. The analysis of these barely translucent, or altogether opaque characters makes up a chapter of Vedic science as difficult as it is important. In any case enough is known to justify the statement that the key-note and engrossing theme of Rig-Vedic thought is worship of the personified powers of nature.

In order to make good this last statement, and at the same time by way of fore-taste of the Rig-Veda, I present here some stanzas of one of its finest hymns.[1] It is addressed to the goddess Ushas, Dawn person-fied, whom the Vedic poets sing with special warmth and liking; the metre imitates the original:

This light hath come, of all the lights the fairest,
The brilliant brightness hath been born, far-shining,
Urged on to prompt the sun-god's shining power.
Night now hath yielded up her place to morning.

The sisters' pathway is the same unending,
Taught by the gods, alternately they tread it.
Fair-shaped, of different forms, and yet one-minded,
Night and Morning clash not, nor yet do linger.

Bright bringer of delights, Dawn shines effulgent,
Wide open she hath thrown for us her portals.
Arousing all the world, she shows us riches,
Dawn hath awakened every living creature.

'T is Heaven's Daughter hath appeared before us,
The maiden dazzling in her brilliant garments.
Thou sovereign mistress of all earthly treasure,
Auspicious Dawn, flash thou to-day upon us !

[1] Rig-Veda I.113 in Professor A. A. Macdonell's translation, in his *History of Sanskrit Literature*, p. 83.   I have taken the liberty of making a few slight alterations.

On heaven's frame she hath shone forth in splendor ;
The goddess hath cast off the robe of darkness.
Awakening the world, with ruddy horses,
Upon her well-yoked chariot Dawn approacheth.

Showering upon it many bounteous blessings,
She spreads her brilliant lustre—all may see her.
Last of the chain of mornings that have passed by,
First of bright morns to come Dawn hath arisen.

Arise ! the breath of life again hath reached us !
Dread darkness slinks away and light is coming !
She hath blazed a pathway for the sun to travel,
We have found the place where men prolong existence.

The Rig-Veda presupposes a tolerably elaborate
and not uninteresting ritual, or scheme of priestly
practices, in connection with the hymns addressed
to the gods. How this may be read between the
lines of the Rig-Veda's poetry I hope to show quite
clearly later on. The Yajur-Veda represents the
exceeding growth of this ritualism, or sacerdotalism,
as time went by. Gradually the main object,
namely, devotion to the gods, is lost sight of : solemn, pompous performance, garnished with lip
service, occupies the centre of the stage. This performance is supposed to have magic or mystic power
of its own, so that its every detail is all-important.
It regulates mechanically the relation of man to the
divine powers by its own intrinsic power, but yet a

power controlled and guided by the wonderful technique of the priests, and their still more wonderful insight into the meaning of all the technical acts. A crowd of priests—seventeen is the largest number —conduct an interminable ceremonial full of symbolic meaning down to its smallest minutiæ. The priests seat themselves on the sacrificial ground strewn with blades of sacred *darbha*-grass, and mark out the altars on which the sacred fires are built. They handle and arrange the utensils and sacrificial substances. And then they proceed to give to the gods of the sacrifice, each his proper oblation and his proper share. Even the least and most trivial act has its stanza or formula, and every utensil is blessed with its own particular blessing. These stanzas and formulas, to which a description of the rites is more or less directly attached, make up the numerous redactions of this Veda.

The Yajur-Veda is a later collection in the main, though it contains much substance that is old, old enough, indeed, to be prehistoric. But like all other Vedic collections, its redaction, at any rate, pre supposes the Rig-Veda. A good many verses of the Rig-Veda reappear in the Yajur-Veda, usually not in the exact form of the Rig-Veda, but taken out of their connection, and altered and adapted to new ends which were foreign to the mind of the original composers. There are also many new verses in the Yajur-Veda which are in the main ritualistic rather than hymnal, concerned with technical details of the sacrifice rather than with the praise of the gods.

But the characteristic element of this Veda are the *yajus*, or formulas in prose, often more or less rhythmic prose. To these this Veda owes its name. They are, by the way, unquestionably the oldest prose on record in the literatures of the Indo-European peoples. These formulas are often brief and concise, mere dedications or swift prayers, accompanying an action, and sometimes hardly addressed to any one in particular. So, for instance, "Thee for Agni" (*agnaye tvā*), or "This to Agni" (*idam agneḥ*), indicate that an object is dedicated to the god Agni. Or, "Thee for strength" is the briefest prayer, or rather magically compelling wish, that the use of a certain article may give strength to the sacrificer. But they swell out from this brevity to long solemn litanies that betray at times such a measure of good sense as may at best be expected in these doings. Often, however, they are sunk in the deepest depths of imbecility, mere verbiage intent upon silly puns on the names of the things used at the sacrifice. When an animal victim is tied to the post the priest addresses the rope with the words, "Do not turn serpent, do not turn viper!"

The Hindus have always had reason to fear serpents; they must have at times been stung by
serpents whom they mistook for ropes, because the
two things are often correlated in their literature.
A Hindu figure of speech (or kenning) for serpent
is "toothed rope."[1] For instance, a theosophic text
of Upanishad character establishes the following
comparison: "As a rope which is not clearly seen
in the dark is mistaken for a serpent, so the un-
enlightened mistake the character of their own
self."[2] That is to say, they do not comprehend the
divine nature of their self. This is sensible, and
there is sense also in the following: Kings are conceived as rulers of the earth. Therefore, at the
ceremony of consecration the king looks down upon
the earth, and prays: "O mother Earth, do not
injure me, nor let me injure thee!" But often
prayer passes over into litany, here as in other
secondary stages of religious literature. The following is an all too typical case: "May life prosper
through the sacrifice! May life's breath prosper
through the sacrifice! May the eye prosper through
the sacrifice! May the ear prosper through the
sacrifice! May the back prosper through the sac-

[1] See the author in *Hymns of the Atharva-Veda* (*Sacred Books of
the East*, vol. xlii.), pp. 147, 368.
[2] Māndūkya-Kārikā, 2. 17. *Cf.* the adage in *Petronius*, 45:
colubra restem non parit, "a serpent does not beget a rope."

rifice!" And finally—O deepest bathos!—"May the
sacrifice prosper through the sacrifice!"[1]

The many thousand formulas of this sort which
occur in the Yajur-Veda and its accessory literature
are now for the first time collected in my Vedic
Concordance. I am sure that the enduring impression which they leave upon the mind, aside from
their partial foolishness, is that of a formalism and
mental decay upon the very brink of dissolution.
The practices which accompany these formulas,
though they contain much that is natural and vigorous, are also covered up by silly details of formalism,
so that it is often difficult to discover their real human
meaning. It is remarkable, however, that new life
springs up on this arid waste. It is as though this
phase of Hindu religion had prepared itself by
its very excesses for a salutary and complacent
hara-kiri. In its last outcome, in the very same
Brahmanical schools where all this folly runs riot,
spring up the Upanishads, those early theosophic
treatises of India which pave the way for her enduring philosophies. The Upanishads in reality, though
not professedly, sweep aside the ritual like cobwebs,
and show the Hindu mind, not yet perfectly trained,
but far from choked; and quite capable of carrying

[1] *Cf.* Winternitz, *Geschichte der Indischen Litteratur*, Part First,
p. 155 *ff.*

on the development of Hindu religions to the really
great results which they eventually reach.

The Sāma-Veda is of all the Vedas the least clear
as regards its origin and purpose. As a literary production it is almost entirely secondary and negative.
The Sāma-Veda is interesting chiefly, because it is the
Veda of music. In addition it contains some original
practices to which tradition has attached a number
of legends unknown in the other Vedic schools.
There are no connected hymns in this Veda, only
more or less detached verses, borrowed in the main
from the Rig-Veda. Even the sense of these verses
is subordinated to the music to which they are set.
The verses are grouped in strophes which, when
accompanied by their music, are known as *sāmāni*,
"melodies." The *sāman*-stanzas are preserved in
three forms. First, in the Rig-Veda, as ordinary
poetry accented in the usual way, and not accompanied by melodies. They are contained mostly in the
first fifty hymns of the first book, and in Books viii
and ix. Most of these stanzas are composed in the
metre *gāyatrī*, or in strophes known as *pragātha*,
which are compounded of *gāyatrī* and *jagatī* verse-
lines. Both the words *gāyatrī* and *pragātha* are
derived from the verb *gai*, "sing," and show
that the stanzas and strophes composed in these
metres were from the start intended to be sung.

Secondly, they occur in the Sāma-Veda itself in a form called *ārcika*, that is, " collection of stanzas." This is a kind of libretto, or text-book containing the stanzas which are to be memorised for "making upon them," as the Hindus say, the *sāman*-melodies. Here also there is a system of accents, peculiar in its notation, but apparently still with reference to the unsung *sāmans*. In the third *sāman*-version, the Gānas[1] or song-books, we find the real *sāmans* as they are to be sung. Here not only the text but also the musical notes are given. Still this is not a complete *sāman* yet. In the middle of the sung stanzas certain phantastic exclamatory syllables are introduced, the so-called *stobhas*, such as *om, hau, hai, hoyi*, or *him;* and at the end of the stanzas certain concluding exclamations, the so-called *nidhanas*, such as *atha, ā, īm*, and *sāt.*[2] They remind us in a way of the Swiss and Tyrolese "yodels" which are introduced into the songs of these countries as a sort of cadenzas, intended to heighten the musical effect.

The Sāma-Veda is devoted a good deal to the worship of Indra, a blustering, braggart god, who

[1] The word *gāna*, again, is derived from the root *gai*, " sing."
[2] The Pancaviṇça Brāhmana relates that the poet Kanva was for a good while puzzled to find a *nidhana* for his *sāman*, until he heard a cat sneeze *ash!* Then he took *ash* for the *nidhana* of his *sāman.*

has to befuddle himself with *soma*, in order to get the necessary courage to slay demons.   He, and he alone, has in the Rig-Veda the epithet *ṛcīshama*, that is, " he for whom the *sāmans* are composed upon the the *ṛks*," or, as we should say, " out of the *ṛks*." [1]   It seems likely that the Sāma-Veda is built up out of remnants of savage Shamanism—the resemblance between the words Sāman and Shamanism, however, is accidental.   Shamanism, as is well known, attempts to influence the natural order of events by shouts, beating of tam-tams, and frantic exhortation of the gods.   The Brahmans were in the habit of blending their own priestly practices and conceptions with a good deal of rough material which they found current among the people.   The *sāman* melodies, too, betray their popular origin in that they seem to have been sung originally at certain popular festivals, especially the solstitial festivals.[2]   The exclamations interspersed among the words of the text are likely to be substitutes for the excited shouts of the Shaman priests of an earlier time.   It is perhaps worth while to note that in later Vedic times the

[1] See my articles, *On Ṛcīshama, an Epithet of Indra*, in *Journal of the American Oriental Society*, vol. xxi., p. 50 *ff.* ; and, *The God Indra and the Sāma-Veda*, in *Vienna Oriental Journal*, vol. xvii., p. 156 *ff.*

[2] See A. Hillebrandt, *Die Sonnenwendfeste in Alt-Indien*, *Festschrift für Konrad Hoffmann*, (Erlangen 1889), pp. 22. *ff* and 34 *ff.* of the reprint.

Sāma-Veda is held in small regard. The Brahmanical law-books prescribe that the recitation of Rig-
Veda and Yajur-Veda must stop whenever the
shout of *sāmans* is heard. One of these law-books,
for instance, counts the barking of dogs, the bray of
asses, the howling of wolves, and the sound of the
sāman as noises so obnoxious or defiling that,
when heard, the study of the other Vedas must
stop.[1]

The interest of the Sāma-Veda for the history
of Hindu religion and literature amounts to very
little. It represents in fact little more than the
secondary employment in the service of religion
of popular music and other quasi-musical noises.
These were developed and refined in the course of
civilisation, and worked into the formal ritual of
Brahmanism in order to add an element of beauty
and emotion. In more modern times the *sāman*-
chants at the sacrifice are said to be quite impressive.[2]

The oldest name of the Atharva-Veda is *atharvāñ-
girasah*, a compound formed of the names of two
semi-mythic families of priests, the Atharvans and
Angirases. At a very early time the former term
was regarded as synonymous with " holy charms," or

---

[1] Compare on this point Professor Ludwig's remark in *Der Rig-
Veda*, vol. v., p. 8.
[2] See the author in the *Vienna Oriental Journal*, vol. xvii., p. 162.

"blessings"; the latter with "witchcraft charms," or "curses." In addition to this name, and the later more conventional name Atharva-Veda, there are two other names, used only in the ritual texts of this Veda. One is *bhṛgvaṅgirasah*, that is, Bhrigus and Angirases. In this the Bhrigus, another ancient family of fire priests, take the place of the Atharvans. The other is Brahma-Veda, probably "Veda of the Brahman," that is the Veda of the supervising fourth priest at the Vedic (*çrauta*) sacrifices.[1] The latter name may, however, be due to some extent to the fact that the Atharva-Veda contains a surprising number of theosophic hymns which deal with the *brahma*, the pantheistic personification of holy thought and its pious utterance. This, as we shall see later on,[2] becomes in time the ultimate religious conception of the Veda.

The Atharvan is a collection of 730 hymns, containing some 6000 stanzas. Aside from its theosophic materials, which look not a little strange in a collection of charms and exorcisms, and some hieratic stanzas which were employed by the Brahman or fourth priest,[3] the collection is almost entirely of a popular character. It consists of hymns and stanzas

---

[1] *Cf.* Caland, *Vienna Oriental Journal*, vol. xiv., p. 115 *ff.*
[2] See below, p. 273.
[3] See Caland in the article just cited.

for the cure of diseases; prayers for health and long life; charms for the prosperity of home and children, cattle and fields; expiatory formulas designed to free from sin and guilt; charms to produce harmony in the life of families and in the deliberations of the village assembly; charms concerned with love and marriage, and, indirectly, with the rivalries and jealousies of men and women in love; conjurations against demons, sorcerers, and enemies; charms for kings in peace and war; and charms calculated to promote the interests of the Brahmans, especially to secure for them the abundant baksheesh for which they clamor with the most refreshing directness.

The Atharva-Veda is of unrivalled importance for the history of superstition, of folk-lore, and popular practices. Related in character are the so-called "House-books" (Grhya-Sūtras). These were composed as formal treatises at a comparatively late Vedic period, yet they report practices and prayers of great antiquity. The Hindus, then as now, took an intensely religious view of their lives. In its even daily course, as well as in its crucial moments, such as birth, investiture, disciplehood, marriage, and death, the life of the Hindu was both sanctified and enlivened by a continuous chain of religious formalities, acts, and festivals. These were codified in the "House-books" with nice minuteness. The Atharva-Veda and the

"House-books" together lay bare with unrivalled preci-
sion of detail the religion of the obscure and the humble. For many a Hindu, through many centuries,
these fond time-honored customs of the fathers,
the *schöne sitte*, was the true religion, which turned
inward, irradiating and sustaining the spirit of a people whose masses live the life of dark toil and do
not see the light revealed to their own elect. To the
development of the higher and ultimate religion of
the Veda these homely practices and superstitions
contribute very little.

Charm against Jaundice.

1. Up to the sun shall go thy heart-ache and thy
jaundice : in the colour of the red bull do we envelop
thee !

2. We envelop thee in red tints, unto long life. May
this person go unscathed, and be free of yellow colour !

3. The cows whose divinity is Rohinī, they who, moreover, are themselves red [*rohinīs*]—in their every form
and every strength we do envelop thee.

4. Into the parrots, into the *ropanākās* (thrush) do we
put thy jaundice ; into the *hāridravas* (yellow wagtail)
do we put thy yellowness.

(*Atharva-Veda*, i. 22.)[1]

[1] See the author, *Hymns of the Atharva-Veda* (*Sacred Books of
the East*, vol. xlii.) p. 7. For the very interesting symbolic practices
that accompany the recital of this charm against jaundice, see p.
263 *ff*. of the same work.

A Woman's Incantation against her Rival.

1. I have taken unto myself her fortune and her glory,
as a wreath off a tree. As a broad-based mountain may
she sit a long time with her parents !

2. This woman shall be subjected to thee as thy bride,
O King Yama (Pluto) : till then let her be fixed to the
house of her mother, or her brother, or her father !

3. This woman shall be the keeper of thy house, O
King Yama : her do we deliver over to thee ! May she
long sit with her parents, until her hair drops from her
head !

4. With the incantation of Asita, of Kaçyapa, and of
Gaya do I cover up thy fortune, as women cover things
within a chest.

(Atharva-Veda, i. 14.) [1]

The poetic stanzas of all sorts, and the ritualistic
prose formulas of the Veda collectively go by the
name of *mantra*, " pious utterance " or " hymn." In
the texts of one group of Yajur-Vedas, the so-called
Black Yajur-Vedas,[2] these stanzas and prose formulas
alternate with descriptive prose chapters which tell
how these *mantras* are to be used at the sacrifice,
and why they are to be used in a given way. The
passages are designated as *brāhmana*. In the case
of the so-called White Yajur-Vedas and also all the
other Vedas the Brāhmanas are compiled into sep-

[1] See the same work, pp. 107 and 252 .ff
[2] For the distinction between Black and White Yajur-Veda see Mac_
donell, *History of Sanskrit Literature*, p. 177.

arate works whose object, again, is to expound the combination of prayer and ritual at the sacrifice. The meaning of the word *brāhmana* is not altogether clear. Either it means " holy practice," or " religious performance " in distinction from *mantra*, "holy utterance," or " religious text." Or, perhaps rather it means the theological explanation by Brahman priests of the religious ritual as a whole, including both prayer and performance. As regards both contents and literary quality, the Brāhmanas are closely analogous to the Hebrew Talmud. In the main they are bulky prose statements of the details of the great Vedic sacrifices, and their theological meaning. Both the performances and their explanation are treated in such a way, and spun out to such length, as to render these works on the whole monuments of tediousness and intrinsic stupidity. And yet the Brāhmanas compel the student of Hinduism that comes to scoff to stay to pray. In the first place they are important because they are written in connected prose—the earliest narrative prose in the entire field of Indo-European speech, only little less archaic than the prose formulas of the Yajur-Veda.[1] They are especially important for syntax : in this respect they represent the old Hindu speech far better than the Rig-Veda, whose syntax and style

[1] See above, p. 33.

are distracted by the licenses and restrictions that go with poetic form. Secondly, the Brāhmanas are an almost inexhaustible mine for the history of the sacrifice, religious practices, and the institutions of priesthood. These institutions in time became so systematic and formidable as to make the names Brahman and Brahmanism typical everywhere for priest and priesthood. Thirdly, the Brāhmana texts not only describe and expound the sacrifice, but they illustrate and enliven it by numerous stories and legends. While engaged in expounding the technicalities of the ritual, they at the same time unconsciously supplement the poetic Vedas. The Hebrew Talmud interrupts the hair-splitting, logic-chopping expositions of its ritual Hallacha, by picking from time to time rare flowers from the garden of its Haggada, or legendary lore. The Brāhmanas no less make drafts upon the past and present of the great storehouse of myths and stories that India has cherished from the beginning of her time. The poetic value of many of these stories may be judged from the fact that they remain stock themes for the Hindu poets of later times.

Here we find, first of all, the story of the flood, wonderfully analogous to the flood legends of all Western Asia, and especially the account of the

book of Genesis.[1] Many echoes are called up by
the story of Cyavana the Bhārgava who, old and
decrepit as a ghost, is pelted with clods by the
children of the neighborhood. Then he punishes
their families by creating discord, so that "father
fought with son, and brother with brother." Cyavana
finally, through the help of the divine physicians,
the Açvins, enters the fountain of youth (*queckbronn*)
and marries the lovely Sukanyā.[2] Like an oasis in
the desert comes the ancient tale of Purūravas and
Urvaçī, whose mythic meaning has been much dis-
puted or altogether denied.[3] Already the Rig-Veda
knows the story, and the Hindu master-poet Kāli-
dāsa, perhaps a thousand years later, derives from it
one of his loveliest dramas. It is a story which contains the same *motif* as the Undine, Melusine, and
Lohengrin stories. A heavenly nymph (Apsaras),
Urvaçī by name, loves and marries King Purūravas,
but she abandons him again because he violates one
of the conditions of this intrinsically ill-assorted

---

[1] See Eggeling's translation of the version of this legend in the
Çatapatha Brāhmana, *Sacred Books of the East*, vol. xii., p. 216 *ff*.
For the story of the flood in general see Usener, *Die Sintflutsagen*
(Bonn, 1899); Andree, *Die Flutsagen* (Brunswick, 1891); and
Winternitz in *Mittheilungen der Anthropologischen Gesellschaft in
Wien*, vol. xxxi (1901), p. 305.

[2] Çatapatha Brāhmana 4. 1. 5. 1 *ff*.

[3] See, last, the author in *Journal of the American Oriental Society*,
vol. xx., p. 180.

union. Not, however, through his own fault, but on
account of a trick played him by the Gandharvas, a
kind of heavenly " sports," the natural mates of the
heavenly nymphs, the Apsarases. He must not be
seen in a state of nudity by his wife. But on a certain
occasion the Gandharvas cause lightning to play:
she sees him and vanishes. Then Purūravas roams
wailing through the land of the Kurus, until he
comes to a lotus pond in which nymphs in the form
of swans disport themselves. One of them is Urvaçī.
They engage in a poetic dialogue which is preserved
without the rest of the story as one of the hymns of
the Rig-Veda (10. 95). This finally relieves the
intolerable situation. The Brāhmana story tells:

"Then she was sorry for him in her heart. And she
spake: 'A year from to-day thou shalt come; then
thou mayest tarry with me one night. Till then thy son
whom I am bearing shall have been born.' And that
night a year he returned. Behold there was a golden
palace. Then they said to him, 'Enter here.' Then they
sent Urvaçī to him. And she spake: 'To-morrow the
Gandharvas will grant thee a wish; choose one.' He
said, 'Choose thou for me.' She advises him to say,
'I desire to become one of you.' The next morning
the Gandharvas grant him a wish. And he says, 'I
wish to become one of you.'"

Then the Gandharvas teach him a particular fire-
offering, by means of which a mortal may become a
Gandharva; thus he becomes a fitting mate for

Urvaçī. Now the reason why this story is preserved is that the Brāhmana text is engaged in describing this very fire-offering; the story proves the magic of this sacrifice which is, aye, powerful enough to turn a mortal into a demi-god.

Here are a couple of short legends, crisp and clear-cut as cameos. They show that, just as the early gods of India are nature-gods, so the early legends are engrossed with problems of nature and the world. The first of these snatches[1] may be entitled

A Legend of the First Pair.

" Yama and Yamī (' the twins ') are the first man and woman. Yama died. The gods sought to console Yamī for the death of Yama. When they asked her she said, ' To-day he hath died.' They said : ' In this way she will never forget him. Let us create night !' Day only at that time existed, not night. The gods created night. Then morrow came into being. Then she forgot him. Hence, they say, ' Days and nights make men forget sorrow.'"

The second legend[2] may be entitled

The Mountains as Winged Birds.

"The mountains are the eldest children of Prajāpati (the Creator). They were winged (birds). They kept flying forth and settling wherever they liked. At that

[1] Maitrāyanī Sanhitā 1. 5. 12.
[2] Maitrāyanī Sanhitā 1. 10. 13. cf. Pischel, Vedische Studien, i., 174 ff.

time this earth was unstable. (God) Indra cut off their
wings. By means of the mountains he made firm the
earth. The wings became clouds. Therefore these
clouds ever hover about the mountains. For this is their
place of origin."

At the end of the Brāhmanas appears a class of
texts known as Āranyakas, or "Forest Treatises."
The meaning of this name is not altogether clear. It
seems probable that these works were recited by
hermits living in the forest, or, more precisely, those
who went to the forest to live, at the time when they
entered the third stage of Hindu life, preparatory
to final emancipation.[1] According to another, less
likely, view they are texts which were taught by
teacher to pupil in the solitude of the forest, rather
than in the profaner surroundings of the town or
village : this because the quiet of the forest
harmonised better with the sanctity of their contents. In either view it is difficult to see why so
much ado should have been made about them. The
Āranyakas are later than the Brāhmanas; this
follows from the position they occupy at the end
of these texts, and from their contents. On top of
descriptions of sacrificial ceremonies we have here
symbolism of the sacrifice and priestly philosophy of
the most fantastic order. The real ritual perform_

[1] See below, p. 288.

4

ance seems for the most part to be supplanted by
allegorical disquisition.   But the themes of the
Āranyakas are by no means of one sort only ; on the
contrary they are heterogeneous and haphazard.
Thus the Taittirīya Āranyaka deals in its first book
with the Ārunaketuka Agni, a particular method of
building the fire-altar ; its second book makes the
rather astounding leap over to Brahmanical educa-
tion and Veda study ; its third, fourth, and fifth
books deal with parts of the Vedic sacrificial cere-
mónial ; and its sixth book describes the old Vedic
funeral ceremonies (*pitṛmedha*).   Still more variegated are the contents of the Aitareya Āranyaka.
What governs the choice of these " forest themes "
escapes our notice almost altogether.   In any case
these books are of lesser importance from the point
of view of Vedic literature and religion, except for the
following fact, which is of paramount importance :

The Āranyakas are symptomatic and transitional.
The important symptom, if we understand the
matter aright, is the subordination of the mere act
of the sacrifice to its allegorical, or, as we might say,
spiritual meaning.   This suppression of the material
side of the ritual bridges over to the last class of
texts which the Veda has to offer along this line of
evolution.   They are the famous Upanishads, the
early philosophical or theosophical texts of India,

which have become fateful for all subsequent higher
Hindu thought. In these the ritual together with
every other manifestation of the religion of works is
negated, sometimes by cautious and delicate innu-
endo, always by the inherent antagonism of the Upanishad themes. The older Upanishads are for the
most part either imbedded in the Āranyakas or,
more frequently, attached to the end of these texts.
From very early times, therefore, they have the
name Vedānta, "End of the Veda."[1] End of the
Veda they are, as regards their position in the redactions of the long line of the so-called revealed
(*çrauta*) texts, and as regards the time of their composition. But they are the end of the Veda in a
higher sense as well. They are the texts of the
Veda's highest religion and philosophy. In particular that system of Brahmanical philosophy which
controls at the present time nearly all the higher
thought of Brahmanical India bears the name
Vedānta. And there is no important form of Hindu
thought, heterodox Buddhism included, which is not
rooted in the Upanishads.

The philosophic and religious quality of the
Upanishads will occupy a good deal of our attention
when we come to the higher religion of the Veda in
the fifth and sixth lectures of this course. For the

[1] Çvetāçvatara Upanishad 6. 22 ; Mundaka Upanishad 3. 2. 6.

present we may content ourselves with some facts in
the literary history of these extraordinary compositions.   As regards their date we can say at least this
much, that the older Upanishads antedate Buddha
and Buddhism.   The production of after-born Upanishads continued, however, many centuries after
Buddhism, into very modern times.   Next to the
Rig-Veda the Upanishads are decidedly the most
important literary document of early India.   For
the history of religion they are even more important.

In the year 1656 the Mogul (Mussalman) Prince
Mohammed Dārā Shukoh invited several Hindu
Pandits from Benares to Delhi, and induced them to
translate the Upanishads into Persian.   Dārā Shukoh
was the oldest son of that Mogul Emperor Shah
Jehān, who built at Agra, as a mausoleum for his
favourite Sultana, the Taj Mahal, perhaps the most
beautiful edifice on earth.   He was afterwards de-
posed from the throne by another son of his, the
bloody and powerful Emperor Aurengzeb.   Dārā
Shukoh was a man of another sort.   He was the
spiritual follower of the famous liberal Emperor
Akbar, and wrote a book intended to reconcile the
religious doctrines of the Hindus and Mohammedans.
Hence his extraordinary desire to spread the knowledge of infidel writings.   Three years after the
accomplishment of the Upanishad translation he was

put to death (1659) by his brother Aurengzeb, on the ground that he was an infidel, dangerous to the established religion of the empire; as a matter of fact, because he was the legitimate successor to the throne of Shah Jehān.[1] India, in more than one respect the land of origins, is also the country from which came the first suggestions of a comparative study of religions. The Buddhist Emperor Açoka, 250 years before Christ, had the spirit of perfect religious freedom. Emperor Akbar, Prince Dārā Shukoh, and Rāja Rammohun Roy are another trifolium of this sort. The last-named enlightened prince wrote in 1824 a book entitled *Against the Idolatry of all Religions;* told the Hindus that caste divisions "are as destructive of national union as of social enjoyment"; expressed belief in the divine authority of Christ; and yet confidently did regard the Upanishads as the true source of the higher religious life of the Hindus. This class of men are the advance guard of the modern scholars who study gentile religions in a spirit of sympathy and fairness.

I would ask you to remember in this connection my friend, the late Professor Max Müller, one of the translators of the Upanishads—Mokshamūlara, as

[1] See Elphinstone, *History of India* (edited by Cowell), p. 610 ; Max Müller, *Sacred Books of the East*, vol. i., p. cvii.

the Hindus called him during his latter days. It happens that *moksha* is the Sanskrit word for "salvation," and *mūla* means "root." To the Hindus his name means "Root-of-salvation," or, as we might say, with a different turn, "Salvation Müller." I do not imagine that Müller believed in the Hindu salvation, which is release from the chain of lives and deaths in the course of transmigration. But if freedom of mind partakes of the flavor of salvation, "Salvation Müller" he was. Max Müller's eminence as a scholar and writer is well known to you; less generally well understood, perhaps, is the liberalising quality of his thought, which he exercised untiringly during more than half a century. Among Europeans he was pre-eminent for the spirit of sympathy and fairness which he brought to the study and criticism of Hindu religious thought.

The Persian pronunciation of the word Upanishad is Oupnekhat. It happened that the Frenchman Anquetil du Perron, the famous pioneer in the study of the Zoroastrian religion of the Parsis, was living in India in 1775. There he became interested in the Persian Oupnekhat, and later on made a Latin translation of Dārā Shukho's version. This was published in Strassburg in two volumes (vol. i. in 1801 ; vol. ii. in 1802). This translation proved eventful in the West. At that comparatively recent

time the Upanishads were yet unknown in Europe.
Notwithstanding its double disguise, first the
Persian, and next the Latin, Anquetil's Latin rendering proved to be the medium through which
Schopenhauer became acquainted with the thought
of the Upanishads. As is well known, Schopenhauer, who is the father of Western pessimism, was
powerfully impregnated with their pantheistic, or,
more precisely, monistic philosophy. His own system is really based upon conceptions that coincide
in one way or another with the more detached
teachings of the Upanishads. Schopenhauer used
to have the Oupnekhat lie open upon his table, and
was in the habit, before going to bed, of performing
his devotions from its pages. His own estimate of
the character of the Oupnekhat is preserved to us
in the following statement: " Next to the original it
is the most rewardful reading possible in the world.
It has been the solace of my life; it will be the
solace of my death." Schopenhauer himself tells us
the reason for his faith in the Upanishads. The
fundamental thought of the Upanishads, he says,
is what has at all times called forth the scoffing of
fools and the unceasing meditation of the wise,
namely, the doctrine of unity; the doctrine that all
plurality is only apparent; that in all individuals of
this world, in whatsoever endless number they

present themselves, one after another, and one be-
side another, there is manifested one and the same
true being.   Therefore the Upanishads are in his
eyes the fruit of the profoundest insight that the
world has ever seen ; almost superhuman thought,
whose authors can scarcely be imagined to have been
mere men.

Schopenhauer unquestionably caught with lynx-
like perspicacity, through the murky medium of the
Oupnekhat, the spirit of the Upanishads, which are
now before us in many editions of their Sanskrit
originals.   It is what is known in philosophy as
monism—the   most   uncompromising,   perfervid
monism that the world has ever seen.   Nor is his
estimate of the religious or philosophical quality of
the Upanishads to be brushed aside lightly.   Professor Deussen, one of the profoundest living
students of Hindu philosophy, himself a trained
philosopher, does not fall far behind Schopenhauer when he says that the thought of the
Upanishads has not its equal in India nor perhaps anywhere else in the world ; that to these
thinkers came, if not the most scientific, yet
the most intimate and immediate insight into
the ultimate mystery of being.   This is not far
behind Schopenhauer's estimate ; both estimates
reflect pretty nearly the position of the Hindus

themselves, who regard the Upanishads as divine revelation.

With all due respect for these great thinkers, I believe that Sanskrit scholars in general incline to a soberer estimate of the Upanishads. With the Hindu view of revelation we need not quarrel. As to the question whether the Upanishads are inspired, we may safely intrust its decision to the broadening spirit of the conception of inspiration, which at the present time is everywhere in evidence in the world. More to the point is, that the Upanishads contain in fact no system of thought, though they did unquestionably inspire later Hindu systematic philosophy. We are often vexed with their unstable, contradictory, and partly foolish statements. The commanding thought of the Upanishads—monism, or the doctrine of unity precedes the Upanishads in the Rig-Veda; unfortunately we do not know by how many years or centuries. Above all, we cannot and should not forget that underneath Upanishad thought, as underneath all advanced Hindu thought, is found the belief in transmigration of souls, a picturesque notion which to the very end retains the quality of folk-lore, rather than the quality of philosophy.[1] But to the Hindus of the Upanishads this belief is an axiom. After all, the prime interest

[1] See below, p 254.

of the Upanishads is literary and historical, We are captivated by the quality of the endeavor more than by the quality of the thing accomplished.

From the literary side the Upanishads captivate not because they are finished products—they are anything but that—but because they show great power and originality as a kind of rhapsodic philosophic prose poems. From the point of view of the history of human thought, what entitles them to enduring respect is that they show us the human mind engaged in the most plucky and earnest search after truth—and let me add that this search is carried on in the sweetest of spirit, without fear of offending established interests, and entirely free from the zealotism that goes with a new intellectual era.

But the Upanishads do not contain consummation. On the contrary, it is the dear, familiar, earnest human fight, doomed rather to disappointment, which very early Hindus here carry on, to find the secret of the world and the secret of self-conscious man in the hiddenmost folds of their own heart—that is what always holds attention, and that is the endearing quality of these texts. Therefore it is true that, wherever the spirit of the Upanishads has been carried there has sprung up genuine human sympathy, if not final intellectual consent. How this is so I shall hope to show later, at the proper point in the development of the religion of the Veda. But for a good while we shall be occupied with more primitive religious forms, though even through these sounds from time to time, almost in the manner of a Wagnerian *leitmotif*, the clarion note of the leading Hindu idea.

LECTURE THE SECOND.

The Hieratic Religion.—The Pantheon of the Veda.

THE religion which is contained in the bulk of the so-called " revealed " (çrauta) Vedic literature, that is in the main body of the hymns of the Rig-Veda, the Yajur-Veda, the Sāma-Veda, and the Brāhmanas, is a hieratic or priestly religion. As regards its mechanism, or its external practices, it is unmistakably liturgic or ritualistic. As regards its immediate purpose, or its economic aspect, it is thoroughly utilitarian and practical. Its purpose is to secure happiness and success, health and long life for man, notably the rich man, while living upon the earth; to secure to a very talented and thrifty class of priest-poets abundant rewards in return for their services in procuring for men this happiness, success, and so on; to satisfy the divine powers, visible and invisible, beneficent and noxious, gods and demons, that is, to establish livable relations between gods and men; and, finally, to secure after death the right to share the paradise of the gods in the company of the pious fathers that have gone there before.

For a generation or two since the real beginnings of the study of the Veda, say fifty years ago, and enduring more faintly to the present day, the imagination of scholars thought it saw in the hymns of the Rig-Veda the earliest spontaneous outbursts of the primitive mind, face to face with the phenomena of nature. The poets of the Rig-Veda were supposed to be simple sons of nature. Awe-struck and reverent, they were supposed to be pondering, without ulterior motive of any kind, the meaning of day and night; of dawn, sun, and moon; of sky, thunder, and lightning; of atmosphere and wind; of earth and fire. The Rig-Veda was the "Aryan Bible," containing the earliest flashes of the religious thought of awakening humanity. This stately gathering of more than a thousand hymns was viewed as a historical collection. Just as the hymns were composed by poets, so the collection and redaction of the Rig-Veda was supposed to have been undertaken by persons of literary taste and redactorial diligence, apparently in order to save these precious monuments for the æsthetic delight of posterity.

One cannot now help wondering to what station in life might have belonged these early poets. I can only think of rhapsodists from out of the people, seized on occasion by the divine frenzy, perchance some village barber—old and semi-religious functionary in the Hindu village—or some village Hans Sachs,

" shoe-

maker and a poet too "

as we may translate the German doggerel.[1] Unless, still less likely, Vedic poetry was the child of the muse of some Rāja's poet laureate, "given to infinite tobacco," eager, as he took the air under one of those huge banyan-trees large enough to hold a village, to bag some good subject for the delectation of the court of his patron. Delightful as might be some such romantic a view to the student of a literature that requires the devotion

---

[1] " Hans Sachs war ein Schuh-
Macher und Poet dazu. "

of a lifetime, it is not the correct view. My own
fancy in the earlier days moved along these lines.
I am not sure but what some such conception of
Vedic literature, faulty as I now believe it to be,
drew me into these studies more enticingly than
could have the soberer view of ripening years.

I shall endeavor later on to attach the right value
to the poetry of the Vedic hymns in the abstract.
I shall also show the way in which these poems express a high quality of religious feeling on the part
of their composers—Rishis, as they are called in the
texts themselves.   My endeavor shall not be to
minimise the quality of these compositions, but
rather to show that they contain the rudiments of a
far higher species of thought than these early poets
could have dreamt of; thought which in its way,
and along its particular avenue, has become final for
all time in India, and even outside of India.   At
present we are engaged with the more external character of the Rig-Veda—its epidermis, as we might say.
The Rig-Veda collection served purely utilitarian
purposes.   It is in fact a prayer-book whose explanation ought not to be undertaken without reference to
definite occasions and definite practices.   The main
body of the books of the Rig-Veda, the so-called family books,[1] represents in all probability the prayers

[1] See above, p. 27.

of different priestly families on the same or similar
occasions, or in connection with the same or similar
sacrifices. The Vedic hymns are not quite described
even if we designate them as sacrificial poetry. It is
a little more than that : I cannot express it better
than by saying, it is the sacrifice—to the gods of
course—treated poetically. In other words these
poems are incidental to the sacrifice. The Vedic
poet rises in the early morning to a sacrificial day.
The very first natural phenomenon he sees with his
own eyes, the glorious maiden Dawn, is at once
pressed into service. She trumpets forth so to say,
to the world that this is going to be a day of sacrifice which shall result in wealth and comforts. The
day goes on, being a mere scaffolding, or ladder upon
whose rungs are placed offerings to the gods. Morning, noon, and evening, tolerably definite gods get
their regular allowance of offerings, and a very admirable kind of hymnal praise, namely the hymns of the
Rig-Veda. As the gods come on, one after another,
or in pairs, or in groups, they enter upon a stage.
The stage is the sacrificial day. They are figures in
a drama, more important collectively than singly.
Take them singly, and I venture to say that even the
Rig-Veda, as does the later ritual, begins to show
most of them in the state of a sort of supernumeraries on the stage of the sacrifice. India is nothing if

not singular. We must not shrink from realising that the earliest Hindu poetry is not epic, nor lyric in the ordinary sense, not idyllic, nor didactic, but that it is almost throughout dominated by a single idea, namely, the praise of the gods in connection with the sacrifice. The sacrifice is the dominant note of Vedic life, as far as it is revealed in these ancient documents. The chief acts of the people living this life, in so far as it is revealed by the literature are sacrificial; their chief thought the praise and conciliation of their gods at the sacrifice. The *soma*, the sacred drink, intoxicates the gods into heroism, or the rich melted butter, or ghee (*ghrta*), that is poured into the willing fire, fattens them into contentment. Especially the *soma* is ever present, in express statement or by implication. So much so that in a technical sense at least the Rig-Veda religion may be designated as a religion of *soma*-practices.

But the hymns are dithyrambic, often turgid and intentionally mystic. It requires at times pretty sharp sight to see, and a clear head to remember, that this poetry hugs the sacrifice closely; that at the bottom of the golden liquid of inspiration there are always the residual dregs of a supposedly useful formalism. In fact the poets, as their fancy flies away from their immediate purpose, succeed uncommonly well in withdrawing the eye from the

5

trivial real properties of the sacrifice to the luminous gods whom they praise so well.

The most beautiful hymns of the Rig-Veda are addressed to Ushas or Aurora, the maiden Dawn, the Goddess Dawn, the daughter of Dyaush Pitar— (Ζεὺς πατήρ), Father Heaven—Homer's Rose-finger Eos. A poet sings her ecstatically:

"We have crossed to the other side of darkness,
  Gleaming Aurora hath prepared the way.
  Delightful as the rhythm of poem,[1] she smiles and shines,
  To happiness her beauteous face aroused us."

                                    (Rig-Veda 1. 92. 6.)

We feel that we are going to be held willing captives of a primitive Shelley or Keats, until we are sobered by another stanza of the same hymn (stanza 5):

" Her bright sheen hath shown itself to us;
  She spreads, and strikes the black dire gloom.
  As one paints the sacrificial post at the sacrifice,
  So hath Heaven's daughter put on her brilliance."

What a comparison! The petty sacrificial post (*svaru*), destined to hold fast an animal victim, gaudily ornamented with paint—it is described technically as having a knob for a head, along with sundry other barbaric beauties—brings us down with a thud from heaven to the mockeries of the

[1] The expression *chándo nd* here and at 8. 7. 36 is to be rendered so, or simply "like a poem." There is no occasion for an adjectival stem *chánda* in the sense of "singer," or the like, as the lexicons and translators generally assume.

sacrifice. Our good friend the poet is after all a monger in technical rites who cannot, even in the moment of his inspiration, quite forget his trade. Lest we think that just this particular poet has nodded for a moment, another hymn repeats the, to us, offensive comparison:

" The bright Dawns have risen in the East,
Like sacrifice posts uplifted at the sacrifice.
Luminous, pure, and clear, they have unbarred
The portals of the stable of darkness."
(Rig-Veda 4. 51. 2.)

We may turn this about the other way and prove the example. Just as it is possible for a brilliant poet of the Rig-Veda to institute comparisons between glorious Dawn and the tawdry sacrifice post, so it is possible for another poet to consider the sacrifice post as a subject fit for high poetic treatment. We are accustomed to make allowance for symbolism in connection with articles belonging to ritual, but I question whether the poets of any other land have ever turned their talents to such curious use:

Rig-Veda 3. 8.

1. " God-serving men, O sovereign of the forest![1]
With heavenly mead at sacrifice anoint thee.

[1] That is, the tree from which the sacrifice post is made.

Grant wealth to us when thou art standing upright,
And when reposing on this Mother's [1] bosom!

2. " Set up in front of the enkindled fire,
        Accepting tireless prayer, that brings strong sons,
        Driving far from us away all noisome sickness,
        Lift thyself up to bring us great good fortune!

4. " Well-robed, enveloped, he is come, the youthful ;
        Springing to life his glory waxeth greater.
        Contemplative in mind and god-adoring,
        Sages of wise intellect upraise him.

9. " Like swans that fly in ordered line
        Have come the pillars gay in brilliant colors.
        They, lifted up on high by sages, eastward,
        Go forth as gods to the gods dwelling-places.

10. " These posts upon the earth, with ornate knobs,
        Seem to the eye like horns of horned cattle.
        Upraised by priests with rival invocations,
        Let them assist us in the rush of battle !

11. " Lord of the world, rise with a hundred branches—
        With thousand branches may *we* rise to greatness—
        Thou whom this hatchet with an edge well whetted
        For great felicity hath brought before us ! "

I am reminded here of the tense struggle in which
my friend the late Professor Max Müller was engaged
with an epithet of Ushas, quite startling, I admit, at
first sight.   The same beautiful Daughter of Heaven,

[1] Mother Earth.

in another hymn, is called Dakshinā. Now the word
dakshinā means "sacrificial fee," or, in plainer words,
it is the baksheesh of the priests at the sacrifice. But
it did not seem tolerable to Müller's poetic mind that
a poet might degrade so charming a theme by such
a comparison:

" Up the shining strands of Dawn have risen,
  Like unto glittering waves of water !
  All paths prepareth she that they be easily traversed ;
  Liberal goddess, kind, she hath become baksheesh."
                                    (Rig-Veda 64. 6. 1.)

The word which I have just rendered by " liberal
goddess " (*maghonī*) is the very one that is used constantly and technically for the patron of the sacrifice
(*maghavan*), the immediate source from which flow
all the fees of the sacrifice. In its feminine form
(*maghonī*) it is used almost solely as an epithet of
Dawn. Here it is, cheek by jowl with *dakshinā*.
Ushas is the patroness of the sacrifice; she is herself
the sacrifice fee, *because she heralds or ushers in the
sacrificial day* [1] after the darkness of the night, when
both liberal and stingy are asleep. If I could get
myself to suspect one of these ancient Rishis of humor, I should say that there was a touch of
humor—anyhow it is unconscious humor—in the

1 See Rig-Veda 7. 78. 3, where the Dawns are said to beget the
Sun, *the sacrifice*, and Agni : *ajījanan sūryaṁ yajñam agnim.*

following appeal to Ushas: " Arouse, O Ushas, liberal
goddess, them that give; the niggards shall sleep
unawakened!"[1] That is to say, what is the use of
waking the stingy man, he is not going to give us anything anyhow. Another stanza states this even more
emphatically: "O shining Dawns, ye liberal god-
desses, do ye to-day suggest to the rich that they shall
give bounty! Let the stingy, unawakened, sleep in
the depths of obscure darkness![2]

The very first hymn in the Rig-Veda that is addressed to Ushas presents in its opening strain the
ritual, serving, economic goddess, in an inextricable
tangle with the poetic divinity. Almost do we feel
that economic advantage and æsthetic delight are
much the same thing to the soul of such a poet:

" With pleasant things for us, O Ushas,
   Shine forth, O Daughter of Heaven,
   With great and brilliant wealth, of which,
   O luminous goddess, thou art the giver!"
                          (Rig-Veda 1. 68. 1.)

And immediately after, in the next stanza, the
significant words, " Arouse thou the benevolence of
our patrons!" And so another time,[3] " To these
nobles give thou glory and fine sons, O patroness
Dawn, to them that have given us gifts that are not

[1] Rig-Veda 1. 124. 10.
[2] Rig-Veda 4. 51. 3.
[3] Rig-Veda 5. 79. 6.

shabby!'" And once again,[1] "God after god urge
thou on to favor us; make all pleasant things come
our way; and, as thou shinest forth, create in us the
inspiration that leads to gain!'" That is to say,
make our poetry so clever that it shall not fail to
stimulate the liberality of the patron of the sacrifice!

We can now understand the *tour de force* of the
poet-priest who, when he sings of Dawn, is anxious
above all that the main issue shall not be neglected.
Therefore he blurts out his crassest thought first,
afflicts the goddess with the doubtfully honorable
title *baksheesh*, and then settles down to a very nice
appreciation of his poetic opportunity:

" Baksheesh's roomy chariot hath been harnessed,
　　And the immortal gods have mounted on it,
　　The friendly Dawn, wide-spread, from out of darkness
　　Has risen up to care for the abode of mortals.

" The mighty goddess arose before all the creatures,
　　She wins the booty and always conquers riches;
　　The Dawn looks forth, young and reviving ever,
　　She came the first here to our morning offering."
　　　　　　　　　　　(Rig-Veda I. 123. 1, 2.)

I think my hearers will understand that it is not
necessary to regard the word *dakshiṇā*, with Professor
Max Müller, as a vague honorific adjective of Dawn,
in the sense of "clever," or the like.[2] Nor need we

[1] Rig-Veda 7. 79. 5.
[2] See his *Auld Lang Syne*, Second Series, p. 223 *ff*.

in this instance to go to the school of the late great
French interpreter of the Rig-Veda, Abel Bergaigne,
who, in a fashion quite his own, transports too many
of the events in the earthly life of the Vedic Hindu
to heaven.   He sees clearly enough that *dakshiṇā*
means "sacrifice fee," and nothing else, but opines
that Dawn is called *dakshiṇā* because she is the gift
of heaven bestowed upon pious men as a recompense
for their piety.[1]   This is all too roundabout, and
unnecessary, and un-Vedic.   Still less can we assent
to the statement of another very sane and enlightened critic of the Vedas, Professor Oldenberg, who
declares that "the hymns to Dawn waft to us the
poetry of the early morn; that they steer clear of
the mystic sophistries of sacrifice technique; and
that they have a charm that is wanting in the sacrificial hymns proper."[2]   Professor Oldenberg takes
the usual view of this interesting goddess.   I would
advocate precisely the opposite view, namely, that
the hymns to Dawn, their many intrinsic beauties
to the contrary notwithstanding, represent the first,
the keenest, so to speak, the least tired sacrificial
mood of these poet-priests as they enter upon the
absorbing business of the day; and that never has
the battledoor and shuttlecock of really fine poetic

---

[1] *La Religion Védique*, vol. i., p. **127** *ff.*
[2] *Die Religion des Veda*, p. 237.

inspiration and plain self-engrossed human neediness been played so frankly and undisguisedly by poet—who must first live and afterwards compose poetry.

Once more I must tax your patience and return to Dawn's epithet *dakshinā*, or "baksheesh." In Rig-Veda 3. 58. 1 Dawn, under the name of Dak-shinā is called the Daughter of Heaven, and Agni, the God of Fire, is called the Son of Dakshinā. What is really meant is, that Agni is the son of Dawn. We have here a double ritual touch which becomes clear only through deep sympathy with the economy of the sacrifice. Why should Agni, " Fire," be the son of Dawn? Is it that Dawn means "light," and light is fire? That would be the far-fetched poetic derivation; I wish to accuse no scholar of having made it. Poetically we think of fire especially as an evening phenomenon, not as a phenomenon of the sober morning. I doubt whether the farmer, as he splits kindling for the breakfast fire of a cold winter morning, cheers himself with the poetic thought that the breakfast fire is the son of Dawn. Our farmers are not temperamentally inclined that way. But it is another matter with the sacrificer who must beautify and beatify all his acts, and throw into them a dash of cajolery. The fact is that the god Agni is also a prized and much extolled divinity of the morning, because the first act of the

sacral day is to kindle the fire that shall convey the
oblations to the other gods.   This is so familiar a
fact of Vedic religion as to require no illustration.
The truly significant thing is, that it creates a theme
in the poetic treatment of the sacrifice, namely:
Agni is the son of Dawn, because immediately after
Goddess Dawn is beheld God Fire is kindled.   In
a beautiful hymn to God Savitar, the motive or
promotive power behind the sun, the doings of the
early morn are described in real poetry:

" Weaving Night hath folded up her woof,
    In the midst of her performance wise Savitar suspends
        her work.
    He riseth from his couch and sets the seasons,
    With fitting plan God Savitar hath come hither."

" The scattered homes and all life
    The mighty flame of household fire pervadeth.
    The largest share the Mother has decreed unto her Son;
    To do his own desire god Savitar hath sped hither."

(Rig-Veda 2. 38. 4, 5.)

Let us not, by any means, imagine that the
Mother here is the unselfish human mother who sees
to it that her boy Devadatta, or whatever his name
may be, has a substantial breakfast.   No, it is the
Mother Dawn whose Son Agni would as a matter of
fact get the largest share anyway, because all oblations are poured into the fire.   We must, I think,

acknowledge that never has sacrifice had such genuine poetry to serve it. But the reverse of the coin is, that never has poetic endowment strayed so far from wholesome theme as to fritter itself away upon the ancient hocus-pocus of the fire-priest and medicine-man. Of course, what finally saves this poetry from banality is the presence in it of those same luminous gods whose brilliance is obscured but not extinguished by such childish treatment.

We are now better prepared to bear up under the statement that Vedic religion is from the very first moment practical and utilitarian, and that the Vedic people, to begin with, practise their religion for what there is in it. The Rig-Veda with its worship of the great nature-gods represents from the start a form of worship very similar, though apparently neither as extensive nor as formal and rigid as the later technical ritual of the Yajur-Vedas and the Brāhmaṇas. The poetry of the Rig-Veda is in the main also really dull and mechanical, but we have seen that, in good part, it is leavened by true beauty of conception, fineness of observation, and all the circumstances of literary composition which we of modern times are accustomed to see at work with its eyes shut—or half shut—to practical considera-tions. We must not be misled by these mental defects of the Vedic poets into an exaggeratedly

pessimistic view of their entire activity. A great
diplomatist, upon whom depends the destiny of his
country, may be shrewd, unscrupulous, Machiavel-
lian, velvet as to glove, iron as to hand, and yet be
a real patriot.   Even so a priestly religion of works,
trivial as these works may appear to our eyes, does
not shut out spiritual elevation.   Nor does practical
poetry shut out entirely the more silent workings of
literary taste and poetic inspiration.   The Vedic
poets themselves insist upon it, their poems are
"well-hewn," "well-fashioned as a war-chariot from
the hands of a skilled artisan."   And so they are in
many cases: if we cut out the foolish sacrifice, and
pare down a pretty thick crust of conventionalism,
there is left in the Vedic hymns enough of beauty
and character to secure them a place in the world's
literature.   Forget but the string that ties the
thought of the Vedic Rishis to the sacrificial post,
and you shall see that thought flit far away to great
heights, where birds do not fly.[1] For the time being,
at least, it becomes what we call inspired, and, anyhow, it breeds the germs that shall flower out to
great things in future days, when Hindu thought
finally emancipates itself from sacrifice along with
many other trivialities of life.

The religion of the Rig-Veda, much like the later

[1] Rig-Veda, I. 155. 5.

hieratic religion of the Yajur-Veda and the Brāhmanas, is the religion of the upper classes.   Even to
this day only rich Brahmanical Hindus are in the
position to perform Vedic sacrifices.   So it was in
olden times.   The popular religion, the religion of
the poor, or of the modest householder, with its
humble rites, and its even more childish reliance
upon sorcery and the medicine-man, runs from the
start side by side with the hieratic religion.   It is
the religion of the Atharva-Veda and the so-called
" House-books."[1]   It happens to lie outside of the
scope of these lectures, though I have for my part
been drawn on by its simple yet tense humanity to
the publication of several volumes.[2]   The religion
of the Rig-Veda presupposes an established household of considerable extent ; a wealthy and liberal
householder ; elaborate and expensive materials ;
and many priests not at all shamefaced about their
fees.

In fact the body of the Rig-Veda presupposes the
ordinary form of the *soma* sacrifice which extends
through an entire day, in the manner of the so-called
jyotishtoma of the later ceremonial.   Or, rather, it
is largely a collection of the hymns composed by vari-

[1] See above p. 41.
[2] For general information on this literature see my book
The Atharva-Veda (Strassburg, 1899).

ous priest families for this important sacrifice. The
soma drink is pressed three times daily : morning,
noon, and evening.   The gods of the Vedic Pantheon
are all interested in these ceremonies ; each has a
fairly definite share in them.   Indra, the god who
figures more frequently than any other, has part in
all three pressings ; but the mid-day pressing belongs
to him exclusively.   Ushas, the Maiden Dawn, and
Agni, God Fire, play, as we have seen, a very
important part in the morning.   The Ādityas [1] and
Rĭbhus, the latter a sort of clever-handed elves,
appear upon the scene in the evening.   A host of
hymns are addressed to pairs of divinities whose
coupling is not always based upon any special
natural affinity between them, but upon purely
liturgic association : Indra and Agni, Indra and
Varuna, Agni and Soma, and so on.

  One important class of hymns, the so-called *āprī*-
hymns, that is, " songs of invitation," consist of
individual stanzas which invoke certain divinities
and personifications of acts and utensils, preliminary to the sacrifice of cattle at the *soma* rites.[2]   God
Fire (Agni) is especially called upon under different,

[1] See below, p. 129.
  [2] See Max Müller, *History of Ancient Sanskrit Literature*, p.
463 *ff*; Roth, *Yāska's Nirukta*, p. xxxvi *ff*; Weber, *Indische
Studien*, x. 89 *ff*; Grassmann, *Translation of the Rig-Veda*, vol. i.,
p. 6 ; Bergaigne, *Journal Asiatique*, 1879, p. 17.

partly mystic designations; of sacrificial articles,
the sacred straw upon which the priests are seated,
the doors of the enclosure within which the offering
takes place, and the sacrificial post to which the
animal is tied have a stanza each in every one of the
ten *āprī*-hymns. These sets of invocations are
purely liturgical; each set belongs to a different
family of Rishis or "seers." In general, each of the
so-called "family books" of the Rig-Veda has its
āprī-hymn. A peculiar odor of sancity, solemnity,
and family pride must have attached itself to these
formulas. In later times, when the hymns of the
Rig-Veda are taken in lump, and employed at the
great sacrifices with but very slight reference to the
particular priest family from which they are supposed to have been derived, the choice of the *āprī*-
hymns is still made according to family. The ritual
books at that time still order that the sacrificer must
choose that *āprī*-hymn which was composed in the
family of the Rishi from whom he would fain derive
his descent.[1] It seems likely, therefore and for
other reasons, that each family book of the Rig-
Veda was intended for essentially the same class of
practices, carried on according to different family
traditions, and to the accompaniment of different

[1] See Çānkhāyana Çrautasūtra 5. 16 ; Āçvalāyana Çrautasūtra 3. 2 ;
Lātyāyana Çrautasūtra 6. 7.

hymns, somewhat in the manner of the later Vedic schools or branches (*çākhā*) of one and the
same Veda.

Large numbers of technical, ritualistic words and
expressions crowd the pages of the Rig-Veda. Its
metres are finished and conventional to a very high
degree ; they are also, to some extent, distributed
among the gods, so that a given metre is associated
especially with a certain god. For instance, the
gāyatrī is the metre of the god Agni ; the *trishtubh*
the metre of the god Indra. They are also distributed
to some extent according to the time of the day :
the *gāyatrī* in the morning, the *trishtubh* at noon,
the *jagatī* at evening. Above all, the advanced
character of the Rig-Veda's ritual manifests itself
in the large number of different designations for
priests. These occur not only singly, but in series :
the names of these priests are largely, though not
entirely, the names of the priests of the later
ceremonial.[1]

And yet the poetry of the Rig-Veda is, in a deeper
sense, original. It is primitive religious poetry, if
by primitive we mean uninterrupted contact with
the last source of its inspiration. The final judgment of its character, after all, depends not so much

[1] See Hillebrandt, *Rituallitteratur*, p. 11 *ff*, and the literature
cited on p. 17 of the same work.

upon the economic motives, or the all-around personal character of its authors as upon the extent and quality of their mental vision. To treat sacrificial themes in the high poetic way seems to most of us hollow mockery. But we must not forget that such performances, to some extent, continue the pious ways of the fathers; that the acts in part symbolise real religious feeling; and that most religions have a trick of throwing a poetic and sentimental glamor around practices that are trivial intrinsically. Then the difference of standards in a semi-barbarous time, such as the time of the Rig-Veda, must count for something. After all that I have said to forefend what may be called a padded or swollen estimate of Rig-Veda poetry and religion, both the poetry and the religion are of singular interest and importance. In its essence the Rig-Veda is not liturgy but mythology. Its priest-poets, in their heart of hearts, are not mere technicians, but tense observers of the great facts and acts of nature, and worshippers of the powers whom they fancy at work in nature. In fact they are both poets and philosophers. There is in this matter some real cause for surprise. We must not forget the long, almost indefinite past of Hindu mythology and religion. I shall endeavor to make this clear in the next lecture when we come to deal with the reconstructions

of comparative mythology. There was plenty of
time for all nature-worship to have stiffened into
mere admiration, fear, and adulation of personal
gods, accompanied inevitably by a more or less complete forgetfulness of the forces in nature from which
sprang the gods. That this was not so is due, in
my opinion, to the vast impressiveness of India's
nature. Its fiercely glowing sun, its terrible yet life-
giving monsoons, the snow-mountain giants of the
north, and its bewilderingly profuse vegetation could
hardly fail to keep obtruding themselves as a revelation of the powers of the already existing gods.
What is still more important, it could hardly fail to
stimulate the creation of new nature-gods to a degree unknown elsewhere. It is this unforgetting
adherence to nature that has made the Vedic hymns
the training-school of the Science of Mythology, and
to a large extent also of the Science of Religion.
Deprived of the hymns of the Rig-Veda, we should
hardly know to this day that mythology is the first
and fundamental adjustment of the individual human life to the outer active, interfering, dynamic
world, which surrounds and influences man from the
moment when he opens his eyes upon the wonders
of its unexplained phenomena. In this sense Vedic
mythology is in its day what empirical science is in
our day.

We can realise this to some extent by calling up
another mythology, that of the Greeks. This is also
based upon nature, but nature is soon forgotten,
or, if not entirely forgotten, much obscured by
after-born movements. Owing to a curious slip,
fortunate from the artistic side, unfortunate from
the religious and mythical side, Greek mythology
fell too completely into the hands of the people.
Poets, artists, and even philosophers handle it, each
in their own way. But there is a notable absence
of those Rishis of the Veda who, with all their too
human sordidness and all their Hindu fancifulness
see the great realities of the world with their eyes
wide open, and work their way slowly but with
secure touch from the single and separate manifestations of nature in the Rig-Veda to the absolute One
Being which is nature as a whole, that is the idea of
unity as finally settled in the Upanishads. The
finest flower of Greek mythology, great Zeus, of
whom Hesiod says, πάντα ἰδὼν ὀφθαλμὸς καὶ
πάντα νοήσας, "The eye of Zeus which sees all and
knows all," or of whom the old Orphic hymn sings,
Ζεὺς ἀρχή, Ζεὺς μέσσα, Διὸς δ'ἐκ πάντα τέτυκται,
"Zeus is the beginning, Zeus is the middle, on Zeus
all is founded," is at the same time the flippant,
breezy Jove to whom the poets ascribe foibles
and vices barely excusable in a modern bon-vivant

and man about town. Too finished personification
causes the break-down of Greek mythology even
from the artistic side. The same poets in whom we
praise above all aversion to everything excessive or
monstrous, those Greek poets who in general fancy
and say just enough, but not too much, run a close
race with the most extravagant fancies of semi-civil-
ised peoples in the description of their primeval
gods. Uranos was maimed by his own son, Kronos;
Kronos, the unnatural son, is also an unnatural
father. For he swallows his own children, and, after
years of tentative but unsuccessful digestion, vomits
forth the whole brood. Fair Phoebus Apollo hangs
Marsyas on a tree and flays him alive. Homicide
without end, parricide and murder of children are
the stock events of their mythology. No wonder
that Plato banished even the Homeric poems from
his ideal republic. And Epicurus had to say: "The
gods are indeed, but they are not as many believe
them to be. Not he is an infidel who denies the
gods of the many, but he that fastens upon the gods
the opinions of the many." Nothing so much as
the complete humanisation of Greek mythology
paved the way for the rapid spread of that Shemitic
religion, deeply ethical in its teachings, Judaeo-
Christianity, among the Indo-European peoples.

You may remember how skilfully Kingsley's novel,

Hypatia pictures Greek religion when it confronts in final struggle, already in the throes of death, the growing belief of the future, as still the Homeric theology; that is, crude anthropomorphism, dashed with occasional but troubled visions of better things. The real rivals of Christianity in the centuries after Christ were Persian forms of religion: Mithraism and Manicheism. Of Mithraism Ernest Renan once said that if the world had not been Christianised it would have been Mithraised; and Manicheism, dualistic, exhaustively Gnostic, with its superb colouring and its appealing asceticism, proved for a time an even more dangerous rival of Christianity.

We know from the history of the later classical Sanskrit literature that India's climate and physiography have kept her poets in touch with nature to a degree unknown elsewhere, until we come to the modern nature poets. Even so, the transparency of the Vedic Pantheon as a whole remains surprising. This results in what we may call arrested personification, or arrested anthropomorphism, and this is the very genius of Vedic religion, and more especially of the religion of the Rig-Veda. Nothing so much as this has enabled the early Hindu thinkers to think out anew, a second and a third time, what had been apparently settled to everybody's final satisfaction,

and was beginning to enter upon a career of rigma-
role.   Thus the Rig-Veda says of God Savitar,
the sun conceived as the promoter of life: " God
Savitar, approaching on the dark blue sky, sustaining
mortals and immortals, comes on his golden chariot,
beholding all the worlds."[1]   It is the fiery ball that
rises from the sea or over the hills, nothing more
in the first place.   The ordinary way of mythology
would be to make of this Savitar a wonderful chari-
oteer, given over, say, to racing or to warlike deeds.
Instead, this process is, as I say, arrested.   The
natural phenomenon remains the repository of renewed and deepening thought.   Even in the Rig-
Veda itself the conception of the sun makes great
onward strides as the most prominent symbol of
the ultimate force at work in the universe.   Another stanza, speaking of Sūrya, another sun-god,
says, " The sun is the Self or Soul of all that
moves or stands."[2]   And yet another, the famous so-called Sāvitrī, or Gāyatrī, which remains
sacro-sanct at all times, and is recited daily even
now by every orthodox Hindu,[3] again turns to
Savitar:

[1] Rig-Veda I. 35. 2.
[2] Rig-Veda I. 115. 1.
[3] See Monier Williams, *Transactions of the Fifth International
Congress of Orientalists*, vol. ii., p. 163 *ff*.

" That lovely glory of Savitar,
   The heavenly god, we contemplate :
   Our pious thoughts he shall promote." [1]

Here is almost the first touch of that inimita-
ble combination of the Upanishads, the Ātman,
"breath," and the Brahma, "holy thought," that is
the combination of physical and spiritual force into
one pantheistic all. As a modern Hindu says of the
Sāvitrī: [2] "It is of course impossible to say what the
author of the Sāvitrī had in view, but his Indian
commentators, both ancient and modern, are as
one in believing that he rose from nature up to
nature's God, and adored that sublime luminary
which is visible only to the eye of reason, and not
the planet we daily see in its course." Kātyāyana
in his Index to the Rig-Veda, the so-called Anu-
kramanī, after stating the familiar classification of
all the gods of the Veda into three types—Agni (fire
and light on earth), Vāyu (air or wind in the atmosphere), and Sūrya (sun in the sky)—proceeds still
farther to assert that there is only one deity,
namely, the "Great Self," (mahān ātmā), and " some
say that he is the sun (sūrya) or that the sun
is he." This is, of course, later thought, Upan-

[4] Rig-Veda 3. 62. 10.
[5] Rājendralālamitra in the Introduction to his Edition of the *Gopatha Brāhmana*, p. 24.

ishad thought, as it appears, for instance, in the Taittirīya Upanishad (8. 8): "He who dwells in man and he who dwells in the sun are one and the same." But this later thought is founded on the repeated revision, so to say, of the conceptions of the sun, fed anew by the sight of this engrossing nature force, which is not obscured and not made trivial by personification into an Olympian, human god.

But we shall return to this all-important matter when we come to the highest outcome of Vedic religion. It is now time to take a look at the individual gods of the Veda, or what we may call the Vedic Pantheon.

THE PANTHEON OF THE VEDA.

At the outset we may observe that this word applies to the Vedic gods only in an analogical sense. There is no Pantheon in the Veda, if by Pantheon we mean an Olympus patterned after a more or less snobbish conception of a royal household, in which every god holds his position and exacts sensitive respect from all the others as the price of his own observance of court proprieties. The Vedic gods have no acknowledged head. They group themselves to some extent according to their characters; for instance, as sun-gods, or storm-gods. As such they have more or less definite habitations.   In the time of the great Epic, the Mahābhārata, no one knows how many hundreds of years later, they really do manage to foregather in the heaven of one of them, namely, Indra's heaven.   They begin to take rank: Indra first, Agni second, and so on.   With that comes a little, very little, of those roseate poetic and plastic possibilities which the poets and artists of all ages have read into the finishedly human Greek Olympus.   We have seen enough of our theme to know that many gods of the Veda are scarcely more than half persons, their other half being an active force of nature.   Such material is not yet ripe even for a Hindu Olympus.   The mind of the Vedic poet is the rationalistic mind of the ruminating philosopher, rather than the artistic mind which reproduces the finished product.   It is engaged too much in reasoning about and constantly altering the wavering shapes of the gods, so that these remain to the end of Vedic time too uncertain in outline, too fluid in substance for the modelling hand of the artist.   On a pinch we could imagine a statue of the most material of the Vedic gods, Indra ; but it is hard to imagine a statue of the god Varuna.   As a matter of fact there is no record of Vedic ikons, or Vedic temples.   In all these senses there is no Vedic Pantheon.

It would seem possible to present the Vedic gods
in the order of their importance, but many are
equally, or nearly equally, important.   We find
nearly a dozen of them engaged in creating the
world, and rather more than a dozen engaged in pro-
ducing the sun, placing it on the sky, or preparing a
path for it ; under these circumstances it is not easy
to rank them.[1] The gods have not all of them come
into existence at the same time. Some belong
to Indo-European times ; others to Indo-Iranian
times.   Of the rest some come from an earlier,
some from a later period of the Veda. If we had
all the dates we might try a chronological arrangement pure and simple, but we do not have all the
dates.

A celebrated ancient Hindu glossographer and
etymologer of the name of Yāska reports three lists,
respectively of 32, 36, and 31 gods, or semi-divine
beings.[2] The last of these seems to begin to tell us
in what succession the Vedic gods appear on the
stage day by day, especially in the morning.[3] He begins well with the Açvins, or " Horsemen " (the Vedic
Dioscuri),[4] Ushas, the Goddess Dawn, and Sūryā,

[1] See Macdonell, *Vedic Mythology*, p. 15.
[2] Nighantu 5. 4–6.
[3] *Cf*. Nirukta 12. 1. Brhaddevatā 2. 7 *ff*.
[4] See below, p. 112.

the "Sun-Maiden."[1]   Soon, however, he grows problematic, or dunder-headed, with Vrishākapāyī, Saranyū, Tvashtar, and so on.   Many years' occupation
with the writings of this worthy, whose sense and
erudition are valued much by the Hindus, as well as
by Western scholars, have not increased my belief
in his authority, or decreased my faith in the infinite possibilities of his ineptitude.   Still this proces-
sion of the gods along the hours of the day has great
interest for the Vedic ritual and the explanation of
the gods themselves.   Touches of it appear in the
hymns themselves, as when the Rig-Veda[2] groups
very neatly the gods of the morning:

"Agni awoke upon the earth, and Sūrya riseth;
  Broad gleaming Dawn hath shone in brilliance.
  The Açvins twain have yoked their car to travel.
  God Savitar hath roused the world in every place."

There is another, more permanent traditional
Hindu division of the gods which arranges them in
three classes, mostly of eleven each, according to
their place or habitat in nature or the cosmos, that
is, in sky, mid-air, and earth.   The classification is
first made in Rig-Veda I. 139. 11 : to some extent it
remains good ever after.   This topography of nature
has a strong hold on the early religion : times without

[1] See below, p. 112.
[2] I. 157. I.

end the later Vedic texts insist that Agni, " Fire "
belongs to, or is typical of the earth ; Vāta or Vāyu,
"Wind," of the mid air, and Sūrya, " Sun," of the sky.[1]
So far it is the philosophy of the obvious. They
continue cleverly along that line in the following
arrangement. I state only the more important
members of each class :

Celestial gods : Dyaus or Dyaush Pitar ("Sky"
or " Father Sky "), Varuna, Mitra, Sūrya and the
Ādityas, Savitar, Pūshan, Vishnu, Ushas, and the
Açvins.[2]

Atmospheric gods : Vāta or Vāyu (" Wind") Indra,
Parjanya, Rudra, and the Maruts.

Terrestrial gods : Prithivī (" Earth"), Agni, and
Soma.

This threefold division, in order to be consistent,
would have to be carried on to the end, so as to include all the gods. As a matter of fact it is uncertain
in many places, even when carried no farther. We
are not so certain as are the Hindus that Indra, for
instance, is a god of the mid-air,[3] even though we
must admire this, on the whole successful, appreciation of the place in nature that belongs to a goodly
proportion of the chief gods.

[1] *Cf.* Brihaddevatā 1. 5 *ff.*
[2] See the index at the end of this book for these and most of the
following gods.
[3] See below, p. 173.

There are yet other possibilities which need not be mentioned, because we shall not follow their lead. Our own course, doubtless open to some objection, will be eclectic. We shall call up the more important Vedic gods under such various points of view as will bring out some one salient quality—which does not say that they may not have other qualities of great interest. Thus the chronological element must remain immensely important. The chronology of the gods must influence to some extent our judgment of this ancient religion of the Veda. The old prehistoric gods that have been imported by the Aryas into India, no matter how much they have been Hinduised, will necessarily have characteristics of their own.

Next come the gods which have been coined in hot haste out of the phenomena of nature in a glowing subtropical climate, or have been imbued anew with the vitality of India's imposing nature. These have not had time to forget their own origin—they are, as I have called them, the gods of arrested personification or arrested anthropomorphism. They are the beacon lights of Vedic religion, of Comparative Mythology, and of the Science of Religion. They are the rare guides and philosophers on this labyrinthine and rocky road ; they have made the Veda the training-school of the study of religion. Since they show in a given number of cases just what has taken place, they point the way when the light becomes hazy.

Again, it is still as true as ever that a large number of the gods, whether early or late, are nature-gods whose origin, we regret to say, has been somewhat obscured by later processes. They again make up for the student of the Veda a class, the most important as well as the most difficult theme of investigation. Every nation's mythology must contain gods of this class. They bring with them problems that will never be dismissed until they are finally answered —and that, paradoxically, may never be. I have in mind gods like Varuna, Indra, and the Açvins. To some Vedic scholars it seems without doubt begging the question to speak of nature-gods in cases when we do not know for certain what was the natural object that was personified. No one can say at this time that the origin of either Varuna, Indra, or the Açvins has been definitely settled. Yet, for my part I confess to that faith, because I remember that such uncertainty represents in truth the normal result of mythologic development. As a rule, a nature-god does not remain transparent for ever: the opposite happens far more frequently, as may be seen, again and again, in Hellenic or Teutonic mythology. Really durable myths are, as a rule, mixed myths, and, therefore, more or less obscure myths. A cer-

tain amount of the complications and entanglements
of human life must be imported into mythology before it becomes mythology. Otherwise it remains
philosophy, primitive cosmic philosophy, or primitive
empirical natural science.

Let me paraphrase a statement made some years
ago in a learned journal.[1] Mythological investigation
must draw a sharp line between the primary attributes of a mythic personage which are the cause of
the personification, and the attributes and events
which are assigned to him or her, and are supposed
to happen after the personification had been com-
pleted. Zeus, as we all know, originally meant "sky,"
and Zeus pater was the personified " Father Sky,"
contrasted with " Mother Earth." But it would be
foolish to search for these primary qualities of Zeus
or the other Greek gods in a play of Euripides, where
the gods are afflicted with all the passions and weak-
nesses of mortal men. Yet he who refuses to myth-
ologise on the basis of Euripides' treatment need not
therefore be sceptical about the naturalistic origin of
most of the Greek gods; he may be willing at the right
time, and in the right stage of the history of any
myth, to point out the physical factors or the physical events which gave it a start. But to be present at the right time, that is not always so easy.

[1] *Journal of the American Oriental Society*, vol. xv., pp. 185, 186.

Further, there are gods in the Veda—not too many in number—about whose origin we can determine nothing that is either definite or helpful. Either these gods have been obscured totally by later events in their natural history, or they are derived from aboriginal tribes or other foreign sources about which we know nothing at all.

Keeping in mind this idea of genesis, we might divide the gods into three classes: transparent, translucent, and opaque gods. And being by nature and occupation philosophically inclined, plagued by an incontinent desire to find last causes, I shall follow the lead of these my suggestions, and describe the gods from the point of view of their origin and the *rationale* of their being under five heads:

1. Prehistoric gods, whether their origin be clear or obscure.

2. Transparent, half-personified gods, who are at the same time nature objects and mythic persons.

3. Translucent gods, who impose upon the investigator the theory of their origin in nature.

4. Opaque gods, who refuse to reveal their origins.

5. To these may be added, as a fifth class, the abstract or symbolic gods who embody an action, a wish, or a fear in the shape of a good or evil divinity,

god, or demon.   Of this class our fifth lecture will
furnish abundant illustration.[1]

Fortunately it does not fall within the province of
these lectures to exhaust the long-drawn and mo-
notonous theme of Vedic mythology, or to establish
definitely the precise origin of all the gods.   My
object is to sketch the motives and principles that
underlie the remarkable chain of religious ideas that
leads from the ritual worship of the great nature-
gods of the Rig-Veda to the high theosophy of the
Upanishads.   Mythology pervades this development to a very great extent, so that we must
understand its principles.   But a mythic figure more
or less cannot materially change the picture, when
once we know how mythic figures in general are
fabricated, and then overlaid with religious feeling
and advancing religious thought.   The particular
character of the individual god soon becomes unimportant.   One of the most remarkable facts in
the religion of the Veda, when carried to its legitimate conclusion, is, that these multiple gods really
vanish in the end, after they have contributed their
individual attributes to the great idea of unity, of
oneness at the root of the universe.   This is the
very negation of mythology and Pantheons; of

[1] See also my essay, *The Symbolic Gods,* in *Studies in Honor of
B. L. Gildersleeve*, p. 37 *ff.*

7

sacrificial hocus-pocus and poetic fable.   And   when
the twilight has engulfed these gods, then, and not
until then, in India as elsewhere, do real religion
and real philosophy begin.

LECTURE THE THIRD.

The Prehistoric Gods.

Two prehistoric periods bearing upon Hindu religion—
Scepticism about Comparative Mythology—Difficulties
in the way of Comparative Mythology—Comparative
Mythology and Ethnology—The myth of Cerberus—
The Indo-European period—Prehistoric words for
god—Father Sky and Mother Earth—The Thunderer
—The Vedic Açvins, or "Horsemen," the two Sons of
Heaven—The Dioscuri in Greek mythology—The
Lettish myth of the two "Sons of God"—Common
kernel of the myth of the two "Sons of Heaven"—
The Aryan, or Indo-Iranian period—Important re-
ligious ideas common to the two peoples—The dual
gods Varuna and Mitra—Ahura Mazda and Varuna—
The conception of $ṛta$, or "cosmic order"—The Adityas
—Aditi, the mother of the Adityas—Mitra, a sun god
—The sun, the moon, and the planets—The Adityas
and Amesha Spents—Early ethical concepts among the
Indo-Europeans—Varuna and Greek Ouranos (Uranus)
—The origin of man—Sundry parents of man—"Father
Manu"—Yama and Yamī, the "Twins"—Interlacing
of the myths of the first man—The human character of
Manu and Yama—Yama, the god of the dead—Soma,
the sacrificial drink of the gods—The myth of Soma
and the Heavenly Eagle—Value of the preceding
reconstructions.

THE treatment of India's prehistoric gods takes on of itself the outer form of a chapter of Comparative Mythology. We have seen in the past that the events which preceded the migration of the Aryas into India belong to two very different prehistoric periods.[1] One of these is the period when the Hindu and Iranian (Persian) peoples, the so-called Aryas, were still one people, a period which does not lie so very far behind the Veda itself, just behind the curtain which separates the earliest historical records of both India and Iran from the very long past which preceded both of them. This is the Indo-Iranian, or Aryan period. The second is the still remoter period of Indo-European unity; the languages, institutions, and religions of this great group of peoples permit us to assume that there was once upon a time one Indo-European people, and that this people possessed religious ideas which were not altogether obliterated from the minds of their descendants, the Indo-Europeans of historical times (Hindus, Persians, Greeks, Romans, Celts, Teutons, Slavs, etc.).

It is my painful duty to report that there has been of recent years a great " slump " in the stock of this subject. In fact, some scholars, critics, and publicists have formally declared bankruptcy against the

[1] See above, p. 13.

methods and results of Comparative Mythology.
In the long run prehistoric reconstructions, infer-
ences, analogies, and guesses do not find favor with
certain types of mind. Of course, it is safer to re-
strict one's self; to analyse and describe the history
of each Indo-European people by itself; and to refrain
from speculating about their connection in a remote
past. Is it not better to stay at home, each trained
scholar in his own philology, rather than to ride out
towards points on the broad and dim horizon which
bounds the more or less hypothetical Indo-European
community, to chase after something that may turn
out to be a mirage ? So it has transpired that what
bid fair once upon a time to grow into an important
branch of historical science is now by some ignored,
if not pooh-poohed. The writings of many great
scholars during the last fifty years or more are now
declared by some to be ready to be wiped off the
slate. It is but fair to note that the same critics
who are sceptical about Comparative Mythology
are, as a rule, inclined also to doubt the explanations
of myths that are restricted to a single people. It
seems to be a matter of temperament, this dislike to
search after origins, after final explanations, after
resolving chords, as it were. Here also they prefer
to treat a myth at its face value, as story, fancy,
poem, and nothing more. Now all this sounds very

virtuous and abstemious; does not the true spirit of research call a halt at the point where rigid mathematic certainty is at an end?

The difficulties which have beset Comparative Mythology are of various sorts: First, the unquestionable delicacy, clear to the point of fragility, of prehistoric materials. Next, the imagination of scholars who incline to such studies is prone, by the very terms of its existence, to be a little excessive. The first results of the science were so striking and fascinating that its development went on too fast, its conclusions became too hasty. May the shades of Theodor Benfey, Adalbert Kuhn, and Max Müller pardon me if I say that their almost poetic genius did at times take flight from the firm earth into sheer cloudland—"where birds can no longer fly." Unquestionably they did compare some mythological names because of the faintest and shakiest phonetic resemblances. Intuitive fanciful explanations of the most complicated myths do to some extent masquerade as scientific results in their writings, and in the writings of the school that grew up mushroom-like about them. A science based upon vague and general resemblances of both things and words could not be otherwise than faulty both as to its details and its philosophic generalizations. In brief, Comparative Mythology suffered from the

pardonably excessive zeal of its early friends. Since
then the pruning knife has kept busy. At the present time this is a subject that should be handled
very gingerly by all those who do not know how to
winnow the chaff from the grain. But there still
is Comparative Mythology, and it is here to stay.

There is yet another difficulty which should be
rated at its right value, not too much and not too little. The primary object of the comparative mythology of the Indo-European peoples is to collect, compare, and sift the religious beliefs of these peoples, so
as to determine what they owned as common property
before their separation. What now, we hear it frequently asked, about the strange peoples, not Indo-
European, nor Aryan, who share these beliefs with
the Indo-Europeans or have similar beliefs? Without
question, in the earlier stages of the science, similarities which were independent products in different
quarters, due to the similar endowment of the human
mind, were confused with genetic similarities. By
genetic similarities I mean such similarities as trans-
mitted mythological conceptions which were already
in vogue among the prehistoric Indo-Europeans, so
that they were continued, with later modifications,
by the separate branches of the Indo-European peoples. Should not, therefore, this entire subject be
handed over to those broader students of Ethnology

.who investigate human customs, institutions, and beliefs all over the world? Does not the entire subject
of the origin and development of religions belong to
Ethnology rather than Philology?

For instance, the Indo-Europeans make much of
the worship of the sun as a supreme being. But so
do the Iroquois Indians, and many other savage or
semi-barbarous peoples. It is indeed true, and it is
an important truth, that the human race, endowed as
it is essentially alike, is liable anywhere and at any
time to incorporate in its beliefs this most imposing
and deifiable visible object in all nature, the sun, the
source of light and heat, seasons and vegetation.
This is the simple ethnological fact. The fact in
Indo-European Comparative Mythology is a different one : it is a historical fact. In the early period
of each Indo-European people heaven, its agents and
powers, including of course the sun, were, as we know
on excellent authority, worshipped or deified. We are
therefore to-day, as formerly, securely intrenched in
the conviction that the worship of heaven and the
visible heavenly phenomena, more or less personal-
ised, did in fact form the common kernel of Indo-
European religion. Now do I fail to see what the
beliefs of other peoples, not Indo-European, along
the same line, have to do with this particular
case, except to show that the Indo-Europeans were

rational beings, and that all the rest of the peoples who worship the sun are, from their primitive point of view, also rational beings.

I have devoted of recent years considerable effort to the statement and explanation of the myth of Cerberus, the dog of Hades. The Veda has two Cerberi, who are said to belong to King Yama. Yama was the first royal man who started the practice of dying. He then went aloft to heaven, and found there, once for all, a choice place where the sons of man might disport themselves after death. There he rules as Yama, the King of Paradise.

The Vedic texts look upon this pair of dogs in a variety of ways. First, the soul of man has to get past them in order to get to heaven. This is the familiar Cerberus idea. Secondly, the two dogs of Yama pick out daily candidates for death. Thirdly, the dogs are entrusted with the care of the souls of the dead on their way to join Yama in heaven. Now we might almost ask with the riddle: "What is it?" I wonder whether there is not present in this audience some ingenious man or woman who can guess what real pair in nature on the way to heaven, coursing like dogs across the heaven, can harmonise these discrepant points of view. But we are not left to guess. The Vedic texts tell us in plain language that they are the sun and the moon, or as they are called, with a very ancient poetic touch, the speckled and the dark. Now the word for speckled is *çabalas;* it fits in well enough with Greek Κέρβερος, considering the susceptibility of mythic proper names to the kind of modulation, or sophistication, which we call popular etymology. But we may disregard the verbal etymology altogether. Other Indo-European peoples have more or less definite notions about one or two dogs. It is more than probable that the early notions of future life turned to the visible heaven with its sun and moon, rather than the topographically unstable and elusive caves and gullies that lead, in the unquestionably late Greek fancy, to a wide-gated Hades. I cannot here afford the time that would be required to the full exposition of this myth, and would refer you to my little book, *Cerberus, the Dog of Hades : The History of an Idea,* published in 1905, which I regard as my program of method in the study of Comparative Mythology. Now, to be sure, we find that other peoples, not Indo-European, here and there, own a dog who gets in the way of the soul on its way to heaven. Obviously, the conception may have arisen independently in the same way : the dead journeying upward to heaven, but interfered with by a coursing heavenly body, the sun or the moon, or both. But grant that somewhere or other a dog, pure and simple, has strayed into this sphere of conceptions without any organic mythological meaning, simply as a baying, hostile, watchdog in heaven or hell. We cannot therefore ignore the wonderful yet simple Indo-European myth which is begotten of high reason and keen appreciation of myth-making opportunity. Plainly, this myth requires no further explanation from the usually vague and half-understood analogies that may be found on the broad ground of universal Ethnology and Folk-lore. Far be it from me to suggest that mythological evidence, whencesoever obtainable, should be excluded from these deliberations: all I want to prevent is the importation of bad coal into Newcastle. Since the Indo-Europeans are one people, let us first study their own minds in their own literature or archeological remains, before turning to the Iroquois, the Papuas, or the inhabitants of the Aleutian Islands for sporadic reports that, more often than not, reach our ear out of their proper connection, or with their point bent. When the smoke shall have cleared there will be—of this I am certain—less airy reliance on ethnological quantities irrational in Indo-European mathematics. But there will be left a goodly stock of Indo-European divinities and simple myths, profoundly interesting, not only with the interest of hoary antiquity, but even more so because they determine and explain the main lines along which move the mythologies of the Indo-European peoples of historical times. The main substance, though by no means the entire substance, of the mythologies and religions of these peoples—this is as true to-day as it was in the days of Benfey, Kuhn and Müller—is the nature myth. If we count Brahmanical theosophy and Buddhism as the two great yields of the study of Hinduism, we may safely add Comparative Mythology as the third great field of religious history that has been opened out by the study of India. Had we but fuller records of ancient Indo-European history and literature, these fuller records would reveal more common myths and religious ideas. The added facts would fill in the necessarily sketchy picture, but it would still be the same picture.

We are by the limits of our plan restricted here to those religious ideas which concern the early religion of India, and even of these we shall select only the more important. We begin with the remoter of the two periods, the Indo-European period.

The universal Indo-European word for " god " was *deivos*, gone over into archaic Latin as *deivos* (*deus*), Celtic *devos* in the Gallic proper name *Devognata*, Old-Scandinavian *tivar*, " gods," Lithuanian *dëvas*, and Sanskrit *devas*. The irreproachable etymology which connects this word with the verb *div*, *dyu*,

"shine," shows that the word came from the luminous manifestations of nature by day and night,
and determines authoritatively the source from
which the Indo-Europeans derived their first and
most pervasive conception of divine power. On
more limited Indo-European territory appears
another general term, Slavic *bogŭ*, Old Persian *baga*
Avestan *bagha* " god," Sanskrit *bhaga* "god of fortune." [1] The word is again of clear origin : it means
"spender of goods, or blessings." It contains the
abstract conception of a good god, embodying an
eternal and never slumbering wish of mankind. The
same eastern region of the Indo-European territory
has in common another sacred word, used as an
attribute of divinity, namely, Avestan (Persian)
spenta, Lithuanian *szventas*, Old Slavic *svętŭ* " pure "
or "holy." This secures for prehistoric religion an
important spiritual concept. Two important conceptions expressing sentiment towards the gods,
that of reverence (Sanskrit *yaj*, Avestan *yaz*, Greek
$\dot{\alpha}\gamma$ in $\ddot{\alpha}\zeta o\mu\alpha\iota$,"revere"), and that of belief (Sanskrit
çraddhā, Latin *credo*, Celtic *cretim*, " believe ") come
from old times, though they need not necessarily
have been in vogue in every part of the territory

[1] The " Phrygian " Zeus Bagaios reported by the Greek glossographer Hesychios is nothing but the Persian Baga ; see the author
in *Transactions of the American Philological Association*, vol. xxxv.,
p. xxxi.

occupied by the Indo-Europeans prior to historic times.

All Indo-Europeans revered the shining sky of daytime as a mighty being. The Hindus, Greeks, and Romans call him respectively *Dyaush pitar*, *Zeus pater* and *Diespiter* or *Jupiter*. The meaning of the name is quite transparent in the Veda, where *dyaus* is still both common and proper noun. It always means sky. The Latin expression *sub Jove frigido*, "under a cold sky," "in a cold climate," preserves the sense of the word as a fossil. The slender myth that is contained here is that of a marital relation between the visible two halves of the cosmos. The lady, or "correspondent" in the affair was "Mother Earth" (Vedic *prithivī mātar*, "terra mater").[1] This union was blessed with children, known frequently in the Veda, and occasionally elsewhere, as the children of the Sky. In the Veda Agni, "Fire," Ushas, "Dawn," and especially the dual "Horsemen," the Açvins, are so named. The "Horsemen," as we shall see later, correspond to the Greek Dioscuri (Διόσκουροι), "Sons of Zeus, or Heaven," Castor and Pollux, and to the "Sons of God" in Lettish mythology. In this instance at

---

[1] Herodotus iv. 59 testifies forthright that the Scythians, closely allied to the Persians, worshipped Earth as the wife of Zeus: Δία τε καὶ Γῆν, νομίζοντες τὴν Γῆν τοῦ Διὸς εἶναι γυναῖκα.

least the concept "children of Father Sky" is prehistoric, and genuinely mythic.

The sky. has another irrepressible quality: it thunders. In this aspect also it became a personal god with a definite name in prehistoric times, who tends at times, as one might naturally suppose, to encroach on the domain of Father Sky, or to blend with him. The chief heathen god of the Lithuanians was Perkunas, "Thunderer," from which is derived the word *perkunyja*, "thunder-storm." The identity of this name with the parents of the Norse "Thunderer," the god Thor (Donar), namely, the male Fjorgynn and the female Fjorgyn, has never been questioned. Here also belongs Parjanya, that most transparent divinity of the rain-storm in the Vedic hymns, who "roars like a lion and thunderous strikes the evil-doers." There is some slight phonetic difficulty here. I would suggest that the word has beer. modulated euphemistically, so as to suggest the idea of "guarding the folk" (*pari*, "about," and *jana*, "folk").[1] Homer's Zeus has absorbed the "Thunderer," and therefore appears in a double aspect. On the one hand he is "far-eyed Sky" ($\varepsilon \dot{v} \rho \dot{v} o \pi \alpha$); on the other he is "cloud-gatherer" ($\nu \varepsilon \varphi \varepsilon \lambda \eta \gamma \varepsilon \rho \dot{\varepsilon} \tau \eta \varsigma$),

---

[1] The original etymology is doubtful ; see Hirt, *Indogermanische Forschungen*, i., 436 ; Kretschmer, *Einleitung in die Geschichte der Griechischen Sprache*, p. 81.

and "rejoices in lightning," or, "twists the light-
ning"($\tau\varepsilon\rho\pi\iota\iota\acute{\varepsilon}\rho\alpha\upsilon\upsilon\sigma\varsigma$). The Lithuanian Perkunas has
absorbed the functions of Zeus and has become chief
god. In the Veda also[1] Parjanya is called " Father
Asura," making him for the moment the double of
Father Sky, the Asura. In another passage he is
even more directly identified with Dyaus.[2]

The Veda has a pair of twin gods, known as
the "two Horsemen" (*açvin*). They are frequently
called "Sons of Heaven" (*divo napātā*). Of all
Vedic divinities they have the most pronounced
mythical and legendary character. They put in
their appearance regularly in the morning, along
with other divinities of morning light. A maiden
by the name of Sūryā, that is "Sun–Maiden," or
daughter of Sūrya, that is " Daughter of the Sun,"
is captivated by the youthful beauty of the Acvins,
chooses them for her husbands, and ascends their
chariot that is drawn by birds. A different yet related touch is added to their character in a riddle-
some brief story[3] which furnishes them with another female relation, namely, a mother by the name

---

[1] Rig-Veda 5. 83. 6.

[2] *Divah parjanyād antarikshāt pṛthivyāḥ.* Vājasaneyi Sanhitā,
18, 55 *et al.*

[3] Told in Rig-Veda 10. 17. 1, 2 ; see the author in *Journal of the
American Oriental Society*, vol. xv., p. 172 *ff.*

of Saranyū. And, once more, with considerable deviation, they figure in a heavenly marriage in which they themselves are not the principals. They are the wooers in a marriage which their own bride Sūryā, according to a later view, enters into with Soma, the Moon. The specific use of the Açvins is that they are the most reliable helpers in need. The hymns harp persistently upon the fact that all sorts of men and women have in the past appealed to them for aid, and have not been disappointed.[1] Even animals are helped or cured by them. In one instance they perform a cure calculated to make green with envy even the most skilled of modern veterinary surgeons, if by any chance he should hear of it. When the racing mare Viçpalā breaks a leg they put an iron one in its place: with that she handily wins the race.[2]

Even the most stalwart sceptics in this field have not found it in their hearts to deny the connection of these divinities and their female relative with the Dioscuri, the " Sons of Zeus," Castor and Pollux (Poludeukes), and their sister Helena. The name of the Açvins' mother Saranyū may, according to a suggestion of Professor E. W. Fay, in its first two syllables contain the sound for sound equivalent

---

[1] See Macdonell, *Vedic Mythology*, p. 51 *ff*.
[2] See Pischel, *Vedische Studien*, vol. i., p. 171 *ff*.

8

of the two first syllables of Helena. The connection
with horses, expressed in the name of the Açvins
(*açva*, "horse"), comes out more strongly with the
Dioscuri, who are celebrated tamers of horses, riders
of horses, and charioteers. The Dioscuri also were
revered as helpers in need, and therefore were called
Anaktes, "protecting lords."

In another quarter, with the Lettish or Baltic
peoples, a strikingly similar myth appears, with the
notable addition that the two "Sons of God" are
mentioned individually as the morning or evening
star. This calls up a feature of the Greek myth:
Zeus rewards the affection of the Dioscuri for one
another by placing them in the heavens either as
morning and evening star, or the twin stars Gemini.
So, to this day, the gigantic statues of the horse-
taming Dioscuri opposite the Quirinal palace in
Rome carry stars on their heads.

A Lithuanian folk-song (*daina*) runs as follows:

> " The Moon did wed the Maiden Sun,
>   In an early day of spring-tide.
>   The Maiden Sun arose betimes,
>   The Moon just then did slink away.

> " He wandered by himself afar,
>   Coquetted with the morning-star.
>   Perkunas hence was greatly wroth ;
>   He cleft him with his sword in twain :

"' Why didst thou thus desert the Sun,
   And wander in the night afar ?
   Why didst thou flirt with the morning-star?
   H̪is heart was filled with grief and pain." [1]

Perkunas is the god of thunder. In the mythology of these peoples he has absorbed the characteristics of the old god of heaven and become the chief
god, just as Zeus, conversely, has taken upon himself the functions of the "Thunderer." This folk-
story presents the materials of the Hindu Açvin
legend in a new arrangement, not at all applicable
to the Hindu myth. But the materials, Sun-
Maiden, Moon, and "Sons of God," are there. In
another folk-song, this time a Lettish one, the
morning-star is represented as pursuing amorously
Saulē, the equivalent of Vedic Sūryā, the "Sun-
Maiden" [2]

With all the rich and often perplexing modula-
tions of this myth, we have the common kernel of a
heavenly dual pair of divinities in intimate relation
with a female divinity of the heavens. The quality
of helpers in need and saviours in trouble is almost
unquestionably begotten of the universal notion that

---

[1] This version of the *daina*, with slight alterations, is that of Professor Chase in *Transactions of the American Philological Association*, vol. xxxi., p. 191.

[2] See Oldenberg, *Die Religion des Veda*, p. 212 *ff*.

the divinities of morning light overcome the hostile powers of darkness. We are not quite so certain as are some excellent scholars that the heavenly pair were originally the morning and evening star, nor has any other naturalistic explanation been proposed which is finally satisfactory.[1] In any case, one of the pair, at least, to which the other has been subordinated, belongs to the events of nature in the morning, and the marriage is with the "Sun-Maiden" (Sūryā, Saulē); or the "Sun Maiden" is imagined to be their sister (Helenà), or even their mother (Saranyū).[2] The myth of which I have given here the merest outline flits about considerably among superficially discrepant notions. It is overlaid with many secondary fancies of the poet and story-teller. No sane scholar will now, as was once the habit, try to make each of the silly "stunts" which the Vedic hymns ascribe to the Açvins part of the organic matter contained in the myth. They are mostly later fancy. And even after deducting the crudities of past interpreters we must not quarrel with certain mental reservations as to this and that detail. But in the last outcome no rational historian or anti-

[1] All explanations have been subjected to searching criticism by Professor Hillebrandt in the third volume of his great work on *Vedic Mythology*, p. 379 *ff*.

[2] In Greek mythology also the Dioscuri are placed in the relation of sons to a mother, namely, Antiope of Bœotia.

quarian will ignore such parallels as shows the
story of the two "Sons of Heaven" with the Hindus, the Greeks, and the Letts,[1] or be so abstemious
as to refrain from looking for reasonable motives
for the creation of a myth that has so marked a
physiognomy.

In brief, once more, there are two luminous sons
of heaven, conceived as horsemen, and as helpers of
men in all kinds of sore straits. They are in loving
relation with another, feminine, heavenly divinity
conceived as a "Sun-Maiden," or "Daughter of the
Sun." This relation is crossed by another affair between the "Sun-Maiden" and the Moon. To conceptions of this sort the Indo–Europeans, before their
separation into the peoples of historical times, had
advanced. The changes and additions to the myth
are not surprising; surprising is, that the myth should
have retained its chief features during great periods of time, in very various surroundings, and under
the constant pressure of a flood of remodelling ideas
poured out upon it by the fertile mind of man, and
tending constantly to obliterate the more primitive
and simple fancies.

I have dwelt before upon the almost romantic interest which attaches itself to the relationship of the

[1] For possible traces of the same myth among the Teutons see De
la Saussaye, *The Religion of the Teutons*, pp. 68 and 140 *ff*.

two peoples, the Hindus and the Iranians.[1] Separated
only by a chain of mountains, they are entirely unconscious of the close relationship of their languages,
literatures, and religions.   Nowhere in the Veda is
there the slightest knowledge of the Avesta ; nowhere
is the Avesta conscious that there is going on across
the Himālaya Mountains in India an intense and characteristic religious development which started with a
good many of the same primitive beliefs as were absorbed by the religion of Zoroaster,   As time went by
the religions of the two peoples became about as different as it is possible for religions of civilised peoples to
be.   On the one side, Parsism or Zoroastrianism, mold-
ed by the mind of a single prophet, Zarathushtra, or
Zoroaster : a dualistic religion, believing in God and
Satan ; an ethical, optimistic, but at the bottom really
unphilosophical religion , yet sufficient, as the modern
Parsis show, to guide a people into a very superior
form of life.   On the other side, higher Hinduism,
monistic, pessimistic, and speculative ; without real
leadership, except that which is present in the own
spirit of each individual bent upon finding the way
out of a hated round of existences through a keen
conviction that there is only one fundamental truth,
the Brahma in the universe and in one's self ;
that, consequently, this world of things is illusory,

[1] See above, p. 13

and must be discarded in order to release from existence.

But these two religions began at approximately the same point, and they continue with enough of the same materials to make the study of each in some measure dependent upon the other. We are here concerned with the Vedic side only. A very considerable number of important Vedic divinities, religious conceptions, and sacred institutions belong to this common Aryan period.[1] Their sphere is enlarged, their meaning better defined, and their chronology shifted across long periods of time, if we keep our eye on the Avesta. Of course we must not neglect to allow for the process of recoining which these ideas have passed through in India. In a certain sense every prehistoric religious idea that has managed to survive and to emerge in India has become Hindu; not the least fascinating part of these researches is to show just how the spirit of India nationalises or individualises the ideas that were born on a different soil.

Two spheres of Vedic ideas and practices concern us here in a particular degree. The first is the sphere of the great Vedic god Varuna, his dual partner

[1] See, Spiegel *Die Arische Periode;* Darmestetter, *Sacred Books of the East,* iv., p. lvi, *ff;* Oldenberg, *Die Religion des Veda,* pp. 26 *ff.,* 341 *ff;* Hillebrandt, *Rituallitteratur,* p. 11, and the bibliographic notes there given; Macdonell, *Vedic Mythology,* p. 7 *ff.*

Mitra, and a set of gods known as Ādityas, to whom belong both Varuna and Mitra. Varuna, unquestionably the most imposing god of the Rig-Veda, is in charge of the moral law or order of the universe, that *rta* which, we have seen, dates at least as far back as 1600 B.C. The second sphere is that of the plant *soma*, which is pressed artfully so as to yield an intoxicating liquor that is accepted joyfully by the Vedic gods as their tipple. It was pressed first by a mythic first man of the name of Yama, and by his divine father Vivasvant. Yama has a sister Yamī, the first pair, who unconventionally people the world. Vivasvant, " the shining one," is the father of Yama, the final progenitor who carries this familiar chain of logic to an end. He is, in all probability, either the "fire," or the " sun "; or, mixedly, "the sun, the divine fire." In each of these spheres Vedic mythology presents itself in its most brilliant aspects. We shall deal with them in the order stated.

In common with most scholars I believe that the god Varuna is to be connected, if not identified, with the chief good and wise god of the Zoroastrian faith, namely Ahura Mazda, or Ormazd, that is " Wise Lord." Varuna carries the title Asura, " Lord," the same word as Ahura; this, however, must not be held to say too much, because other gods of the Veda are honoured with the same distinguishing title. But Varuna is a close partner in a partnership which is expressed in the dual number. It consists of himself and the god Mitra, who is, however, little more than a silent partner in the combination. Such partnerships are frequent in the Veda, but exceedingly rare in the Persian Avesta. Yet the Avesta, in a matter-of-fact manner, joins Ahura and Mithra in the same dual partnership as the Veda does Varuna and Mitra.[1] Since Ahura is the paramount divinity of the Avesta his pairing with Mithra has every appearance of a fossil, left over from a time when Ahura's supremacy had not yet become absolute, in other words, from a time when Ahura and Mithra were on a par of dignity. It seems to me an almost unimaginable feat of scepticism to doubt the original identity of the two pairs. Ahura figures, however, by himself also. Again, it seems unlikely that Ahura Mazda, when mentioned by himself, is not the same Ahura that appears in the combination Ahura and Mithra, because Ahura Mazda, taken by himself, is so very like Varuna, the Vedic partner of Mitra. In the Zoroastrian system Ahura Mazda orders the world, and assigns to all good creatures and entities their respective places and activities. Ahura creates the divine order (*asha*), the good waters and plants,

[1] See Spiegel, *Die Arische Periode*, p. 185 *ff*.

light, earth, and all that is good.   He was the first
progenitor, the first father of divine order.   He
made a way for the sun and the stars.   It is he that
causes the moon to grow or wane.[1]   As guardian of
divine order Ahura is not to be deceived, does not
sleep; he sees all human deeds, overt or covert.[2]

The Veda describes Varuna in the same spirit, at
times in almost the same words.   He is the sup-
porter of beings; he has spread the atmosphere over
the forests; has put fleetness into the steed, and
milk into the cows.   He has placed intelligence into
the heart, fire into the waters, the sun upon the sky,
the *soma*-plant upon the mountains.   He has opened
a path for the sun; the floods of the rivers hasten
seaward like racers obeying the divine order.[3]   Even
more pointed than Ahura's is the expression of
Varuna's omniscience and undeceivableness: he sees
all the past and all the future; he is present as a
third wherever two men secretly scheme ; his spies
do not close their eyes.

The hymn Atharva-Veda 4. 16 presents a rugged
picture of Varuna in his rôle of omniscient and
omnipotent god:

[1] Yasna 37. 1; 44. 3.
[2] Yasna 31. 13 ; 43. 6 ; 45. 4 ; Vendidad 19-20. *Cf.* Oldenberg in
Journal of the German Oriental Society, vol. i, p. 48.
[3] Rig-Veda 5. 85. 2 ; 87. 1 ; 8. 41. 5.

" The great guardian among these gods sees as if from anear. He that thinketh he is moving stealthily—all this the gods know.

" Whoso stands, walks, or sneaks about, and whoso goes slinking off, whoso runs to cover ;—if two sit together and scheme, King Varuna is there as the third and knows it.

" Both this earth here belongs to King Varuna and also yonder broad sky, whose bounds are far away. The two oceans are Varuna's loins ; yea, in this petty drop of water is he hidden.

" Whoso should flee beyond the heavens far away would yet not be free from King Varuna. From the sky his spies come hither ; with a thousand eyes they do watch over the earth.

" All this King Varuna does behold—what is between the two firmaments, what beyond. Numbered of him are the winkings of men's eyes. As a (winning) gamester puts down the dice, thus does he establish these (laws)."

Another hymn, Rig-Veda 7. 86, depicts Varuna as guardian of moral order, hence angry at the misdeeds of men. The contrite attitude of his suppliant, a singer of the family of the Vasishthas, the authors of the seventh book of the Rig-Veda, has a strong Hebraic flavor, and, like the preceding hymn, suggests many a passage of the Psalms :

1.

"Wise, truly, and great is his own nature,
Who held asunder spacious earth and heaven.
He pressed the sky, the broad and lofty, upward,
Aye, spread the stars, and spread the earth out broadly.

2.

" With my own self I hold communion :
How shall I ever with Varuna find refuge?
Will he without a grudge accept my offering ?
When may I joyous look and find him gracious ?

3.

" Fain to discover this my sin, I question,
I go to those who know, and ask of them.
The self-same story they all in concert tell me ;
' God Varuna it is whom thou hast angered.'

4.

" What was my chief offence, O Varuna,
That thou wouldst slay thy friend who sings thy praises?
Tell me, infallible Lord, of noble nature,
That I may be prompt to quench thy wrath with homage !

5.

" Loose us from sins committed by our fathers,
From all those, too, which we ourselves committed !
Loose us, as thieves are loosed that lifted cattle ;
As from a calf, take off Vasishtha's fetters !

6.

" 'T was not my own sense, Varuna!   'T was deception,
'T was scant thought, strong drink, or dice, or passion.
The old are there to lead astray the younger,
Nay, sleep itself provokes unrighteous actions.

7.

" Let me do service to the merciful giver,
The zealous god, like a slave, but sinless !
The gracious god gave wisdom to the foolish,
He leads the wise, himself more wise, to riches.

8.

" May this our song, O Varuna, we pray thee,
Reach to thy heart, O god of lofty nature !
On home and work do thou bestow well-being ;
Protect us, gods, for evermore with blessings !"

We are accustomed to make much allowance for
general similarities in the conceptions of the gods of
different peoples, but it is scarcely possible that they
should reach so far.   The connection that exists between Ahura Mazda and Varuna is expressed, however, not only through their general similarity as
supreme arbiters of the world and its moral law.
That very particular conception, which dignifies
alike Veda and Avesta, namely, Vedic *ṛta*, Avestan
asha (*areta*), and Cuneiform Persian *arta*, is, of course,
not entirely put in the keep of those two gods.   But

it is theirs in an especial degree. One of the most interesting parallels between Veda and Avesta is that both gods are described as the "spring of the *rta*, or righteousness." Varuna is *khā rtasya* (Rig-Veda 2. 28. 5) ; Ahura Mazda *ashahe khāo*, (Yasna 10. 4). The words are sound for sound the same. The high thought of the *rta* is in many ways similar to the Confucian idea of order, harmony, and absence of disturbance. It is unquestionably the best conception that has been elaborated by the Aryans.

We have seen [1] that it reaches back at least to 1600 B.C., and yet, notwithstanding its early date, it is superior to any of the earlier conceptions of the remaining Indo-European peoples. As far as the Veda is concerned, it presents itself under the threefold aspect of cosmic order, correct and fitting cult of the gods, and moral conduct of man. [2] We have in connection with the *rta* a pretty complete System of Ethics, a kind of Counsel of Perfection.

As the basis of cosmic order the *rta* rules the world and nature. The established facts of the visible world, but especially the events of nature that recur periodically, are fixed or regulated by *rta*. Those

---

[1] Above, p. 12.

[2] The same threefold character is quite evident in the Avestan *asha*. See Mills *Journal of the American Oriental Society*, vol. xx., pp. 31 *ff*., 277 *ff*.

daughters of heaven, the Maidens Dawn, shine upon
the morning sky in harmony with $ṛta$, or when they
wake up in the morning they rise from the seat of $ṛta$.
The sun is placed upon the sky in obedience to the
$ṛta$. He is called the wheel of $ṛta$ with twelve spokes.
This means that he courses across the sky as the year
of twelve months. Even the shallow mystery that
the red, raw cow yields white, cooked milk is "the $ṛta$
of the cow guided by the $ṛta$."[1] The gods themselves are born of the $ṛta$ or in the $ṛta$ ($ṛtajāta$);
they show by their acts that they know the $ṛta$,
observe the $ṛta$, and love the $ṛta$.[2]

The religion of the Veda, as we have observed, rests
upon the material foundation of cult and sacrifice.
These performances are not always regarded merely
as merchandise wherewith to traffic for the blessings
of the gods. They begin to evolve intrinsic virtues
and harmonies. In a later time, the time of the Yajur-
Vedas, as we have seen,[3] the technical acts of the
sacrifice are imbued with magic and divine power.
But even in the Rig-Veda the sacrifice fire is kindled
under the "yoking of the $ṛta$," or, as we should say,
under the auspices of world order. Agni, the god of

---

[1] "O sage mir, wie geht es zu,
     Giebt weisse milch die rote Kuh?" *German nursery rhyme.*

[2] *ṛtajñā, ṛtāyu, ṛtasap,* and so on.

[3] Above, p. 31.

fire, is " scion of the *ṛta*," or " first-born of the *ṛta*."
He performs his work with *ṛta*, carries oblations to
the gods " on the path of *ṛta*."   Prayers, lowing like
cattle, " longing for the *soma*-drink," take effect in
accordance with *ṛta*.[1]   A figure of speech, bold to
the point of grotesqueness, turns prayer into " *ṛta*-
fluid, distilled by the tongue."[2]   Holy sacrifice, in
distinction from foul magic, is performed with
ṛta : " I call upon the gods, undefiled by witchcraft.
With *ṛta* I perform my work, carry out my thought."
Thus exclaims a poetic mind conscious of its own
rectitude.[3]

Finally in man's activity the *ṛta* manifests itself as
the moral law.   Here it takes by the hand the closely
kindred idea of truth, *satya*.   Untruth, on the other
hand, is *anṛta*, more rarely *asatya*, the same two words
with prefix of negation.   The two words *satya* and
anṛta form a close dual compound, " truth and lie,"
" sincerity and falsehood," both zealously watched
over by God Varuna.[4]   They remain the standard
words for these twin opposites for all Hindu time.
Varuna is the real trustee of the *ṛta*.   When God Agni
struggles towards the *ṛta* he is said in a remarkable
passage to become for the time being God Varuna.[5]

[1] Rig-Veda 9. 94. 2.   [2] *Ibid.*, 9. 75. 2.
[3] *Ibid.*, 7. 34. 8.   [4] *Ibid.*, 7. 49. 3.
[5] *Ibid.*, 10. 8. 5.

Truth and lie include, by an easy transition, right and wrong-doing. In a famous hymn[1] Yamī (Eve) invites Yama (Adam) to incestuous intercourse. Mythically speaking this is, of course, unavoidable: they are the first pair, and there are no other human beings whatsoever. But the poet conceives of the situation in the spirit of his own time. When Yamī pretends to justify the act Yama exclaims pithily: "In saying the *ṛta* we shall really say the *anṛta*," which, rendered more broadly, means to say: "When we pretend to justify the act as being *ṛta*, 'right-doing,' we really shall knowingly engage in *anṛta*, 'wrong-doing.'" We may imagine Yama finally saying: "Anyhow, don't let us beat the devil about the stump!"

Varuna and Mitra, the dual pair, are implicated still further in a group of divinities of the name *āditya*. The number of these gods is very uncertain. Sometimes it is three: Mitra and Varuna, with Aryaman as third. This third god, no less than the first two, is Indo-Iranian: the name of Aryaman's Avestan counterpart is Airyama. The name of this not too determinate god seems to mean "comrade"; accordingly Aryaman figures in the Veda as the typical groomsman at the wedding rites. Beyond this triad the name *āditya* becomes very indefinite,

[1] Rig-Veda 10. 10.

9

both as to number and the individuals which it is supposed to harbor. As regards number, the god Indra sometimes swells the three to four. Then there is seven, a favourite and vague number; to this the legendary Mārtānda[1] (Indra) is at times added as eighth. In later times the number rises to twelve. Not more than six are ever mentioned by name outright in the Veda: Bhaga, Daksha, and Ança in addition to the three mentioned above. Bhaga, "Fortune," is not only Indo-Iranian, but even Indo-European, as we have seen.[1] Ança, " Portion," "Apportioner," is a very faint abstraction. And so is Daksha, " Dexterity," " Cleverness."

Now the Veda conceives of the Ādityas as the descendants of a feminine Aditi who cuts a considerable figure as a very abstract female, suggesting the ideas of " freedom from fetters," " freedom from guilt," " boundlessness," and " universe." She is finally identified in the Hindu mind with " earth." A father who might be responsible for the offspring of this interesting lady is never mentioned. We are struck first of all with the fact that Aditi, the mother, a purely Hindu product, is obviously younger than her own sons, the best of whom are at least as old as the Indo-Iranian period. I have, for my part little

[1] See Macdonell, *Vedic Mythology*, p. 43.
[2] Above, p. 109.

doubt but what Aditi is a well-executed abstraction of some kind. In the past I have suggested[1] that the word *āditya* meant originally " of yore," and that this set of antique gods whose most substantial members are prehistoric were thus fitly named " gods of yore " or " gods of old." We may perhaps contrast with this the description of Indra as " later born " (*anujāvara*), in a legend told in Taittirīya Brāhmana (2.2.10). From the word *āditya*, conceived as a metronymic, the feminine Aditi might be easily abstracted. If this is well taken we must assume that the Veda had forgotten the meaning of *āditya* in the sense of " of yore." This was necessarily the case before some speculative genius might invent the mother Aditi. Another explanation, that of Professor Macdonell,[2] has perhaps the advantage of greater simplicity. He starts from the expression *aditeḥ putrāḥ*, which is applied several times to the Ādityas. This, he thinks, may have meant originally " sons of freedom," perhaps better " sons of guiltlessness " ; such an expression may have led to the personification of Aditi as a female mother of Ādityas. At all events Aditi may be safely re garded as later drippings from the very sappy

---

[1] See my essay, *The Symbolic Gods*, in *Studies in Honor of B. L. Gildersleeve*, p. 45.

[2] *Vedic Mythology*, p. 122.

myth of Varuna and the Ādityas. The interpretation of Aditi as " boundlessness," or " universe," sits very well upon an assumed mother of these great gods. Aditi is later defined as " earth," a narrowing of her scope, somewhat as we of the modern languages make synonymous the terms " world " and " earth." [1]

The mythic cycle represented by Mitra-Mithra and Varuna–Ahura is important for early Vedic religion, and, more permanently, for the whole history of Persian religion. There is no chapter of Aryan religion and mythology that has stimulated the instinct of ultimate interpretation more persistently than this very one. I am of those who cannot imagine any cessation of these attempts for any great length of time. The one solid point in the genesis of these myths is the solar character of the Aryan Mitra. In later Persian the word *mithra* in the form *mihir* is the name of the sun. As previously stated,[2] this solar Mithras passed, in the centuries after Christ, out of the bounds of Persia and started upon a career of conquest which threatened at one time to subject all Western civilisation.

[1] See the author in *Zeitschrift der Deutschen Morgenländischen Gesellschaft*, xlviii., 552, note ; Macdonell, *Vedic Mythology*, p. 125.
[2] Above, p. 85.

Now what is the natural origin of that other
partner in the dual partnership, namely, Vedic Varuna the Asura, Avestan Ahura Mazda? Not very
many years ago Professor Oldenberg advanced and
defended ingeniously the hypothesis [1] that Varuna is
the Moon, and this theory he did not hesitate to
follow to a very logical conclusion. Mitra and
Varuna are Sun and Moon. They are members, as
we have seen, in a group of gods called Ādityas.
Oldenberg chooses, perhaps a little hastily, the
number seven as the sum total of this group.[2] Similarly in the Avesta, Ahura is accompanied by the so-
called " Immortal Holy Ones," the Amesha Spents,
the angels of the Puritan Zoroastrian faith. They
also make up the number seven. Mithra, we may
note, is altogether absent from the Avestan arrangement. Now Oldenberg believes not only that
Varuna and Mitra were the Moon and the Sun, but
that the Ādityas, essentially identical with the
Amesha Spents, were the planets. He assumes still
further that the whole set, originally, were not Indo-
European divinities at all, but that they were borrowed by the Aryans from a Shemitic people—
presumably the Babylonians—far enough advanced

---

[1] See his latest treatment of the matter in *Zeitschrift der Deutschen Morgenländischen Gesellschaft*, vol. l., p. 43 *ff.*

[2] See above, p. 129.

in astronomical knowledge to observe the interrelations of sun, moon, and the planets.

The Ādityas and the Amesha Spents have been compared often, perhaps over-confidently. It is not necessary, in order to feel unconvinced by Professor Oldenberg's chain of consequences, to deny a certain nebulous cluster of ancillary or subsidiary divinities which hovered about the persons of the supreme Indo-Iranian twin-gods Ahura-Mithra, Varuna-Mitra. As a matter of fact the Amesha Spents are not the Ādityas. I do not believe that the Ādityas, indefinite in number and gradual in their development in India, represent that cluster, or even its very gradual Hindu substitutes. Several Ādityas, notably Mitra, Bhaga, and Aryaman recur in the Avesta, but are not listed as Amesha Spents. Either Macdonell's or my own hypothesis [1] as to the origin of the Ādityas presupposes that their origin as a class of gods is gradual and secondary. The Amesha Spents, on the other hand, are sheer abstractions. I confess that there is not in me the faith to see in them anything as concrete as personified planets. The mere names of the " Immortal Holy Ones " show what I mean. They are: Vohu Manah, " Good Mind "; Asha Vahishta, " Best Righteousness "; Khshathra Vairya, " Wished-for Kingdom," or

[1] See above, p. 131.

"Good Kingdom"; Spenta Armaiti, "Holy Har—mony"; Haurvatāt, "Soundness," "Health"; and Ameretat, "Immortality." It is a beautiful, heavenly hierarchy, but it is unmythological, non-naturalistic to the bone. If anywhere, then here is the place where sprang up purely symbolic gods in the man-ner of the symbolic creations in Bunyan's *Pilgrim's Progress.*

As for the Shemitic source of this deified solar system, Professor Oldenberg, if I understand him aright, is in part led thereto by the striking ethical character which is manifested by the gods of this group at so early a period of Indo–European history as is the common period of Persia and India. He thinks that the Shemites preceded the Indo–Euro-peans in the evolution of ethical concepts, and that the ethical coloring of the Ahura–Varuna myth came along with the divinities themselves. But, as I have shown, we find the chief Aryan ethical concept, the *ṛta*, safely imbedded in the Persian dynastic Arta-names that are reported in the Cunei-form Tel-el-Amarna tablets, 1600 years B.C. Now that date lies far back of the period from which Pro-fessor Oldenberg would deduce his results. I should prefer to judge that the wide prevalence of this idea at a very early date shows rather that some, if not all, Indo-Europeans had advanced in ethical

perception at an earlier date than has hitherto been
suspected, at a date when the Shemites had not as yet
evolved any ethical ideas of quite as fine a flavor
as the *ṛta*.

Professor Oldenberg is not the only scholar to
whom Varuna has suggested the moon. Yet I think
that this interpretation, when taken outside of that
hypothesis which involves the entire solar system,
has not very much in its favor beyond the close
dualic connection of Varuna with Mitra, the sun. I
confess, moreover, that I am not quite willing to
listen to any interpretation of this god which leaves
out in the cold Greek Οὐρανός. There has been
some phonetic scepticism about the equation
varuṇas = οὐρανός which time has not justified. Greek
οὐρανός is Indo-European *u̯oru-n̥nos* or *u̯oru-enos;*
Sanskrit *varuṇas* is Indo-European *u̯oru-nos*. The
two forms differ no more than, for instance, Vedic
nūtanas and *nūtnas*, "recent," or Greek στεγανός
and στεγνός, "covered." Here is a situation met with
quite often in this kind of inquiry. The interpretation of the myth is, as usual, not quite certain.
Few interpretations of advanced myths are quite
certain. Next, the etymology, like that of many
etymologies of mythic proper names, likewise brings
with it no bonded guaranty. The next step
is, that they who do not believe in the interpre-

tation are prone to belittle the etymology. But
there is little gain in pooh-poohing an etymology which will not stay pooh-poohed. The time
will never be when any interpretation that disre-
gards this obvious comparison will pass current
free from perplexity and misgivings. All settle-
ments that do not regard it will be temporary
and doomed in the end to be repudiated. It
would seem to me that we must accept this important etymology, and submit to its guidance. It
shows that Varuna belongs not only to the Indo-
Iranian (Aryan) time, but reaches back to the
Indo-European time, and that he represents, on
the impeccable testimony of οὐρανός, some aspect
of the heavens, probably the encompassing sky, in
accordance with the stem *uoru* which is its essential
element. Rig-Veda 8. 41. 3 states that Varuna, the
distinguished god, embraces the all, and Rig-Veda
I. 50. 6 states that Mitra (the sun) is the eye of
Varuna. The dualism of Heaven and its eye, the
sun, is not less well taken than the dualism sun and
moon.

Into the gusty discussion which has grown up in
a particular degree around this point of interpretation I would lead my hearers no farther. There is
perhaps not a single point in the comparative study of
this most important sphere of Aryan religion which

is lifted entirely above doubt. I have endeavored to give a conservative estimate of the varying interpretations, as free from fanciful exaggeration of the probabilities as it is from unwholesome scepticism.

We may now turn to the second great sphere of Indo-Iranian mythology. It deals with the first men and sacrificers, and the *soma*-liquor, the most distinguished sacrifice to the gods.

One of the duties of primitive man as he grows into the irksome habit of looking for the reason of things is to find a reason for himself. He does not take himself for granted, but assumes that he originated from something or other. This is as a rule not as easy as it is in the myth of Deucalion. All that he had to do was to throw stones, the bones of Mother Earth, behind him, and, behold, there were men. The abstract benevolent Divinity turning himself into a creative Father God is not always at hand; he does not on the whole represent a very primitive form of thought, certainly not in India. An important and widespread conception, partly religious in character, is Totemism. This is founded on the belief that the human race, or, more frequently, that given clans and families derive their descent from animals: totemic names like " Bear " and " Wolf " carry traces of this sort of belief into our time. This particular question is a splendid theme of universal ethnology, but I have never been able to discover that it has any considerable bearing upon the ancient religion of India. The many hints at its possible importance should be substantiated by a larger and clearer body of facts than seems at present available.[1]

We have met previously the greatest parents of them all: Heaven and Earth. Their union was conceived in early Indo-European times as the fruitful source of the heavenly gods. Occasionally they shoulder the additional responsibility for the human race as well. In the Indo-Iranian period there was a personage, Vedic Vivasvant, Avestan Vīvanhvant, who figures rather paradoxically as the father of the first men, Yama and Manu. He is, as the Vedic texts state distinctly and intelligently, the Sun conceived as the Father of men.[2] God Agni, " Fire," is occasionally regarded as the progenitor of men.[3] There is in this some vague symbolic connection with the process of obtaining fire by friction. This is the Vedic process: the two sticks which are rubbed are conceived as parents; Agni is their child, the first progeny, and, next, possibly, the first man. Certainly the epithet *āyú*, " living," is used, on a large scale,

---

[1] *Cf.* Oldenberg, *Die Religion des Veda*, p. 68 *ff.*
[2] See Hillebrandt, *Vedische Mythologie*, vol. i., p. 488 *ff.*
[3] Rig-Veda 1.96.2; 10.53.6.

of fire and man alike. It continues, or seems to continue, a sense of the relationship of Agni and man. [1]

Now the Veda discloses, and all Hindu tradition harps upon, a father of the human race by the name of Manu, or Manush Pitar, "Father Manu." The word *manu* is nothing else than our own word " man ": there is good reason to believe that this " original man " was set up as a kind of Adam or Noah in Indo-European times. [2] For a while the primitive mind seems to be well content with this eponymous man: later on, as I shall presently show, Manu is in his turn duly furnished with a well-established father, Vivasvant, about whose origin people have ceased to worry.

From a later time, yet still a very early time, namely, the Indo-Iranian period, comes the Vedic myth of Yama, the son of Vivasvant. This myth is the clearest and best-preserved common piece of property of the two religions. As to the component ideas of this myth I see no room for doubt. Yama means "twin." He is the male of the obligatory twin pair that is required to people the world in real earnest. The female Yamī, little as is said about her in the earlier parts of the myth, plays Eve to Yama's

[1] See Bergaigne, *La Religion Védique*, vol. i., p. 59 *ff*.

[2] Compare Tacitus, *Germania*, chapter 2 : " They [the Germans] honor Tuisto, a god who has sprung from the earth, and his son Mannus, as the originators and founders of the race."

Adam. She is, however, not Yama's bone, but his independent, self-poised sister. As a truthful historian I have been compelled to record that Yamī, like Eve, was the prime mover in the nefarious but necessary act of peopling the world.

Both Manu and Yama are primarily nothing but first men. Yama's father Vivasvant is probably primarily the sun, whose divine character is, however, at that time quite completely forgotten: old as is this affiliation it is probably not original, because the first twins, Yama and Yamī, are in reality an attempt to beg the question of the origin of the human race altogether. The descent of man from the sun represents another start towards solving the difficulty; of course this conception must and does blend with the Yama pair. In the same way Manu begins quite early to adopt Vivasvant for his father, and he remains so for all time. The myths begin to interlace very much, and to sprout shoots in unexpected directions. A famous pair of riddle-stanzas, Rig-Veda 10. 17. 1 and 2, expand the theme in an interesting fashion, according to an interpretation which I have proposed[1]: it is worth while to present it as an extreme example of the blend of original mythic roots into a real myth:

Tvashtar, the creator, offers his daughter Saranyū

[1] *Journal of the American Oriental Society*, xv., 172 *ff*.

in marriage to the whole world of gods and mortals.
The suitor who gains favor is Vivasvant, conceived
as a mortal. Saranyū, barely wedded, is displeased
with Vivasvant and flees; not, however, until she
had given birth to the twins Yama and Yamī. This
marriage, you perceive, provides the twins with a
mother, whereas they have previously had only a
father. In order to make sure her escape, she
changes into a mare and flees to the gods, who hide
her away from her mortal family, Vivasvant, Yama,
and Yamī. The gods, in order to make matters
still more safe, construct another female, called Savarnā, who is to take Saranyū's place in Vivasvant's
affections. The word *savarṇā* means "of like character"; it trickily states that the new female was at
one and the same time like Saranyū in appearance,
and also suitable in character to the mortal Vivasvant—more suitable than the divine Saranyū, we
may perhaps understand. Vivasvant begets Manu
with the Savarnā, and thus Manu comes into possession both of a father and mother. Ultimately
Vivasvant finds out the deception practised upon
him, follows Saranyū in the shape of a horse,[1]
and thus gaining her favor, begets with her the
Açvins, "the Horsemen" or Dioscuri. Saranyū
abandons them also, just as she has previously

[1] *Cf.* the classical Pasiphaë myth.

abandoned the twins Yama and Yamī, and resumes, we may understand, her independent station as a divinity.

The final outcome of these mythic entanglements are two progenitors of the human race: Yama the son of Vivasvant, and Manu the son of Vivasvant. They remind us in a way of Adam and Noah, especially as Manu is the hero of the Hindu flood-legend, which is astonishingly like the account of the book of Genesis. Vivasvant and his double progeny all of them are endowed for a good while with purely human qualities. According as the profane or sacred interest preponderates these first, and, of course, great men become kings or great sacrificers of yore. Manu is the typical first sacrificer. The later sacrificer of the time of the Veda, as he performs on his sacrificial place, fancies himself a Manu, doing like Manu (*manuṣvat*), in the house of Manu. In the Avesta Vīvanhvant is the first mortal who pressed the drink *haoma* (*soma*) in behalf of the corporeal world. His son Yima and his descendants continued to do so, but Yima turns rather into a worldly ruler, the king of a golden age, in which there is nor old age nor death; nor heat nor cold; nor want nor disease. He becomes the leading Epic personality in later Persian times. In the Avesta he is called " Ruler Yima," Yima Khshaeta; this expression turns in later Persian into Djemshed, the well-known hero of the Persian Epic, the *Shah Nameh*, or *Book of Kings*; the name is now familiar to Western readers as the interlocutor in Omar Khayyam's *Rubayat*.

The myth takes another, even more important turn in the Veda. Yama is the first mortal king who died and found for the race of men a heaven where they may rejoice in the company of the pious dead, especially those pious archpriests of mythical antiquity, the Angiras. He is the first of mortals who died and went forth to this heaven [1]: "Where is Vivasvant's son, the king, where is heaven's firm abode, where are yonder flowing waters, there let me live immortal." [2] "He (Yama) went before and found a dwelling from which no power can shut us out. Our fathers of old have travelled the path: it leads every earth-born mortal thither. There, in the midst of the highest heaven, beams unfading light, and eternal waters flow; there every wish is fulfilled on the rich meadows of Yama." "These blessed have left behind them the decrepitude of their bodies; they are not lame nor crooked of limb." [3]

[1] Atharva-Veda 18. 3. 13.
[2] Rig-Veda 9. 113. 8.
[3] Atharva-Veda 3. 28. 5; 6. 120. 3.

Yet this same Yama, such is the terror of death, becomes in due time the Hindu Pluto, god of hell and judge of the wicked. Which shows how important is the special and national treatment of myths, and how constant is the disregard of what may be called the radical beginnings of myths. From Yama of the golden age of man to dread Yama, the destroyer of the bodies of men—as such he figures in the later Pantheon of the Mahābhārata—Comparative Mythology traces every step.

And now, the sacrificial substance which, when freely given to the gods, secures to mortals the golden age of the Avesta and the paradise of the Veda is the old Indo-Iranian drink, Vedic *soma*, Avestan *haoma*. It is an accepted fact with each people that this drink was prepared from a plant of the same name; that it was an intoxicating drink; and that it was regarded as the tipple of the gods, inspiring them to those valorous deeds which men craved of them. Physically, it is a plant that grows upon the mountains, has green shoots, and yields a golden fluid which insures health and long life and averts death. No wonder that Haoma-Soma is king of the plants, and that the pressing and offering of it was an important act. After pressing it was purified through a sieve of hair and mixed with milk—doubtless the earliest milk-punch on record. The

Rig-Veda and the Avesta report the names of the same ancient worthies that prepared the fluid for the gods: Vedic Vivasvant, Yama, and Trita Āptya; Avestan Vīvanhvant, Yima, Āthwya and Thrita. This marks the most intimate, if not the most important, relation between the two religious literatures.

Mythically, this wonderful drink was conceived as coming from heaven, the type on earth of the heavenly fluid that is hidden in the clouds. In the Veda a heavenly eagle, doubtless the lightning, breaks through the brazen castle, the cloud, within which the heavenly fluid is confined, and carries it off to earth, that is, causes it to pour down upon the earth. It is the simple phenomenon of cloud, lightning, and downpour of refreshing and life-giving rain which is turned into the heavenly prototype of this delightful drink.[1]

The Iranian *haoma* is also fetched from heaven by a bird, though the manner of his descent to earth is not told. In both literatures the drink finally turns god, slays demons, casts missiles, and gains in his perfect wisdom[2] light for

---

[1] See the author in *Journal of the American Oriental Society*, xvi., 1 *ff*. For analogous conceptions in Greek mythology, see Usener in *Rheinisches Museum*, lx., 24 *ff*. For winged lightning see Jacobsthal, *Der Blitz in der Orientalischen und Griechischen Kunst*, p. 19, 25 *ff*, 36 *ff*., 42.

[2] Vedic *sukratu* = Avestan *hukhratu*.

men, "the best world of the pious, the luminous world."

In the Avesta the *haoma* practices and worship are somewhat fossilised: its use has become secondary and symbolic. In the Veda *soma* figures as the most distinguished offering, the champagne of the gods, which exhilarates them and inspires them to valorous deeds against demons and the enemies of the liberal sacrificer. Herculean Indra especially stands in need of an especial meed of courage in his demon fights; therefore he is the most insatiable consumer of "pools of *soma*," as the texts say. He has his very own allowance at noontide; the rest of the gods, including Indra, come in at the other nodal points of the day, morning and evening. The entire ninth book of the Rig-Veda tells of the sacred practice of brewing this Bacchanalian drink; it praises the drink itself as a god in poetic and ecstatic language. We may remember that the hieratic parts of the Rig-Veda are preoccupied with the dispensal of *soma* to such an extent that, in a sacral sense of least, we may speak of the religion of the *r̥caḥ* as a religion of *soma* rites.

I have tried with as secure a touch as in my power to sketch some of the principal myths and religious ideas which the Vedic Hindus preserved out of the long past which preceded their occupation of India.

I am mindful of the relative insecurity of prehistoric reconstructions: they must, in the nature of the case, to some extent be prehistoric guesses. Nevertheless, in handling these specimens, and remembering others which time forbids me to treat here, my own faith at least in the reality of these very old fossils of human thought has grown and not shrunk. When I say human I mean, too, that they are so very human. They are of the logic of mental events. The effect upon the higher grade of primitive mind which the facts and events of the visible world may naturally be expected to have—that is the effect which we have traced. We must, of course, not imagine either Indo-Europeans or Indo-Iranians as town folk, but rather as semi-barbarous nomad and agricultural tribes, accustomed to look hard, and to be strongly interested in the sights that nature offers. Certainly if our analyses are not true they are well found: Father Sky and Mother Earth; next, the inevitable children of Father Sky, namely, the visible bodies and luminous phenomena on the sky, the *deivōs*, "or shiners," as the most persistent idea of the early gods; their destruction of hostile darkness; their character as overseers and guardians of cosmic and moral order; thunder, the commanding voice of another little less obvious god in heaven :— they appear treated with simplicity and directness, we may say with inevitable logic. The perplexed search after a first man, a first pair; the propagation of man; and man's destiny after death is more subjective, yet carried out with clever realism. There is no better way until we come to the clarified, yet intrinsically no less impotent philosophies of a much later time. Because all these myths, fancies, poems, and chains of logic are founded on the outer universe and on human consciousness, therefore we are reasonably sure that they are real. This is an even more valuable guaranty than philological exactness and historical sense which, of course, should strengthen the hands of the trained investigator in every detail. In my opinion the mental sanity of Comparative Mythology is its brief to practise the profession of a true science; and it is permissible to say with renewed emphasis that the religion of the Veda is the child in direct succession of the prehistoric ideas which this science calls out from the dim past.

LECTURE THE FOURTH.

The Transparent, Translucent, and Opaque Gods.—Religious Conceptions and Religious Feeling in the Veda.

The transparent gods: their importance for the study of
   religion—Father Sky and Daughter Dawn—Sūrya, a
   god of the sun—Vāta and Vāyu, gods of wind—The
   most transparent god: Agni, Fire—Agni as the sacrifice
   fire—Prehistoric gods of fire—Birth and youth of Agni
   —Agni as god of the morning—New births of Agni—
   Agni on the altar, the agent of the gods—Priesthood
   and divinity of Agni—A hymn to Agni—Other myths
   of the Fire God—The translucent gods: definition of
   the term—God Vishnu—God Pūshan—God Indra, as
   an example of an opaque god—Traditional explanation
   of the myth of Indra and Vritra — Professor Hillebrandt's interpretation of the same myth—Renewed
   definition of the religion of the Rig-Veda—Renewed
   definition of Vedic practicalities—Conflicting prayers
   and sacrifices—The conception of faith—Faith related
   to Truth and Wisdom—Faith personified—Faith and
   works—The reward for faith postponed to heaven—
   Contrast between early "faith" (çraddhā) and later
   "devotion" (bhakti)—"Gift-praises," another sop to
   the sacrificer—The religious feeling of the Rig-Veda—
   The utilitarian sense—The glory of the gods—Absence

of real sentiment towards the gods—Poetic inspiration
the true religious feeling—The complacent master-
singers—The poets' own estimate of their work—The
divine quality of devotion.

FOR my part I always come to this theme in the
spirit of scientific elation. You know from
preceding statements what I mean by transparent
gods. They are the gods who are at one and the
same time nature object and person. In other
words, they are mythic formations whose personification is arrested by the continued action and the
vivid memory of the very qualities which lead to
personification. Figuratively speaking, just when
the chemical is about to precipitate or to crystalise
into something unrecognisable, and far removed
from its elements, it is shaken and dissolved anew.
We are spared the labor of a qualitative and quanti-
tative analysis. In the midst of the uncertainties and
intricacies of this subject as a whole the assurance
that these processes be renews the courage of the
investigator. There is hope that out of the Babel
of discordant opinions, many of them grown on the
soil of just scepticism, the gods and the beliefs of
ethnic religions will reveal their origins. I believe
that, next to the Science of Language, the Science
of Religion is the clearest of mental or historical
sciences, for the very reason that it is possible to

trace some of the most advanced products of religious thought to simple and tangible beginnings
in nature and in human consciousness.

Comparative mythology has influenced these
studies profoundly by extending the field and the
time within which we may carry on our observations.
At the risk of seeming too insistent, let me point
out once more, how it has spanned the distance between prehistoric "Father Sky" and the strenuous
human personality of the Olympian Zeus of the
poets. Now a visit to the Vedic Pantheon brings us
into the very workshop where the gods are made.

We have encountered before some transparent
gods. "Father Sky" (Dyaush Pitar), who comes
from olden times, and does not grow in the Veda
into anything like the personality of Greek Zeus
Pater, but is there submerged by other formations
that have gained ground at his expense. We have
seen what his daughter Ushas is : Eternally young
and beautiful, ageless in distinction from the wither-
ing race of man, she appears as a lovely maiden dis-
playing her charms to the world. While doing this
she caters at the same time to interests which are the
reverse of poetic. She starts the day of sacrifice, her
face set towards very practical performances. She
secures rewards for pious men and their agents with
the gods, namely the priests. Yet, on the whole, the

poetic possibilities of this loveliest of nature sights
gain the day.   She releases from service her sister
Night as she rises from the darkened East higher
and higher to flood heaven and earth with her waves
of light.   To the Sun-God she is a bride, opens for
him her bosom's splendor.   Or, she loves the two
Açvins, the Dioscuri, with whom she travels on their
car drawn by birds., Divine and gracious maiden,
but yet no more than one of nature's splendors, she
is the type of many a heaven-born story, could we
but read it aright.

Next Sūrya (Sol, Helios) appears upon the stage.
He is the Sun-God treated as transparently as possible.   He is styled the son of Dyaus, the Father
Sky ; Dawn is his bride, or, in another mood, the
Dawns are said to be his mothers.   On a car drawn
by seven tawny steeds, his course is guided by other
great gods, the old Ādityas, Mitra, Varuna and
Aryaman. Again, he is the eye of Mitra, Varuna, or
Agni (Fire).   He is the preserver and soul of all creation, of everything that stands or moves.   Enlivened
by him men pursue their vocations.   He is far-see-
ing, man-beholding, takes note of the good and bad
deeds of mortals.   They in turn look up to him,
rejoicing in the security and the inspiration which
his light affords.

I shall let speak for itself the hymn, Rig-Veda

1.50, in the attractive metrical translation (with slight changes) of the late Dr. John Muir; see his *Original Sanskrit Texts*, vol. v., p. 160, and *Metrical Translations from Sanskrit Writers*, p. 179:

Hymn to Sūrya

By lustrous heralds led on high,
The fire Sun ascends the sky;
His glory draweth every eye.

The stars which gleamed throughout the night,
Now scared, like thieves slink fast away,
Quenched by the splendor of thy ray.

Thy beams to men thy presence show;
Like blazing fires they seem to glow.

Conspicuous, rapid, source of light,
Thou makest all the welkin bright.

In sight of gods and mortal eyes,
In sight of heaven thou scalest the skies.

O fiery God, with thy keen eye,
Thou scannest, like God Varuna,
The doings of all busy men.

Thou stridest o'er the sky's broad space,
Thy rays do measure out our days;
Thine eye all living things surveys.

Seven tawny steeds thy chariot bear,
Self-yoked, athwart the fields of air,
Bright Sūrya, god with flaming hair.

That glow above the darkness we
Beholding upward soar to thee,
For there among the gods thy light
Supreme is seen, divinely bright.

And there are other gods, not a few, whose origin
in nature is positively on the surface. So the two
wind-gods Vāta and Vāyu, the former of whom,
on the likely evidence of Teutonic Wotan-Odhin,
is probably prehistoric. A good bit of profound
human philosophy is contained in the mere fact that
Vāta is described as a real person in language such
as that of the following hymn,[1] and that he may
finally be invited to partake of oblations :

Hymn to Vāta

Now Vāta's chariot's greatness ! Breaking goes it,
And thunderous is its noise. To heaven it touches,
Makes light lurid, and whirls the dust upon the
    earth.

Then rush together all the blasts of Vāta :
To him they come as women to their trysting ;
With them conjoint, on the same chariot travelling,
Hastes the god, the king of all creation.

Sleepless hastes he on his pathway through the air,
Companion of the watery flood. First-born and
    holy,

[1] Rig-Veda 10.168, reproduced with some changes from Professor
Hopkins's translation, *The Religion's of India*, p. 88.

> Whence, forsooth, arose he, and whence was he
> created?

> The breath of gods and source of life is Vāta.
> This god doth journey whithersoe'er he listeth,
> His sound is heard but no one sees his figure.
> With our oblation let us this Vāta honor!

But there is one figure that looms far above all others in ancient Hindu religious history from Veda to Mahābhārata, as the classical illustration of how a phenomenon of nature may be itself and personal god at one and the same time. It is the god Agni "Fire," who is element and god at the beginning and remains so to the end. Richard Wagner adopts in the Nibelungen tetralogy the doubtful interpretation of the Norse god Loge (Loki) as fire; Wotan calls upon this red-haired, impish god to appear when he wishes to hedge with fire his erring child Brunhilde. This is interesting, because it shows how even the modern poetic fancy may get itself to bridge over, uncritically, as behooves the poet, the great gap that is between the reality of nature and the unstable speculation of myth-makers. Native Hindu theologians in their scholastic mood find time to worry over the fact that a god like Agni can be devouring element and intelligent god at one and the same time. Even the Epic poet in the Mahābhārata stops to wonder: "There is but *one* Agni, yet is he kindled manifold ";[1] and Agni himself is made to say: " Because I can multiply myself by the power of mental concentration (*yoga*), therefore am I present in the bodies (of men, as vital fire)."[2]

Agni is, next to Indra, the most prominent god of the Rig-Veda, quantitatively speaking. He is the theme of more than two hundred hymns, and owes his special prominence to the personification of the sacred fire which is present at all Vedic performances. In the hieratic (in distinction from the popular) hymns of the Rig-Veda there will be few cases in which Agni is not more or less directly connected with the sacrifice. And it is well now to take this simple article, the sacrifice fire, and let it unfold its own story step by step. How it turns in the hands of these priestly poets into a person gifted with the thinly disguised qualities of fire ; into a messenger mediating between men and gods; into an archpriest typical of holy rites; and finally into a god. But to the end, as we shall show, the origin of all these ideas is never forgotten ; the god remains a more or less well-assorted bundle of fire qualities and fire epithets. Therefore, too, he remains to the

[1] Mahābhārata 3. 134.8＝10658.
[2] *Ibid.*, 1. 7. 6＝916.

last an indifferent vehicle for far-reaching speculations, or the finer sort of religious feeling.

The Sanskrit word *agnis*, " fire," at all events, is Indo-European; Latin *ignis*, Lithuanian *ugnis*, Old Slavic *ogni*. Some kind of worship of the sacrifice fire, and with it some degree of personification, is likely to have taken place in Indo-European times. The Greeks and Romans, as well as the Aryans, offered libations to the fire when using it to convey offerings to their gods.   But there was no definite result that we know of ; the chaste figure of Hestia of the Greeks, or Vesta of the Romans, contrasted with boisterous male Agni, shows that the initial conception must have been faint and unstable, to enable it to produce shapes so thoroughly diverse. In the main God Agni is in every essential a product of the poet-priests of the Rig-Veda.

In India, as elsewhere, fire was produced by friction, and this mode of starting fire was obligatory as far as the sacrifice fire was concerned. The two fire-sticks, or drills, called *araṇī*, are therefore Agni's parents, the upper stick being the male, the lower the female. They produce him under the name of Āyu " Living " ; wonderful to narrate, from the dry wood the god is born living. At once he becomes the type of human progeny, and faintly figures as, or suggests the first man and the originator of the

human race.[1] The new-born infant is hard to catch;
he is born of a mother who cannot give him
suck. The child as soon as born devours the
parents.

With a different touch, because powerful exertion
is required to produce Agni by friction, he is frequently called " Son of Strength."

The pronounced ritualist quality of the poetry of
the Rig-Veda fixes Agni as a divinity of the morning, rather than of the night. Interpretations of Rig-
Veda passages which involve reference to something
like the cosy family hearth, the tea-kettle simmering,
the wind soughing outside, are generally moonshine.
Nor is his definite association with the morning just
what we should expect it to be from our point of
view; no suggestion, perchance, of the merry dairy-
maid milking the cows, or the housewife busy with
a comfortable breakfast. Familiar, home-life touches
are not absent altogether even in the Rig-Veda;
they are more abundant in the " House-books "
(Grhya-Sūtras). But in the main Agni is cosmic
and ritualistic, and little else. He dispels the darkness, destroys the demons of night. He throws
open the gates of darkness; earth and sky are seen
when Agni is born in the morning. He is even

[1] See above, p. 139.

supposed to lift daily the eternally youthful sun to the sky to furnish light to the people.[1]

Such is his cosmic aspect in the morning. On the other hand his ritualistic character betrays itself in his epithet *usharbudh*, which means "waking at dawn." We have seen before that he is also regarded as the son of Dawn.[2] All this emphasises the opening of the sacrificial day, ushered in by the Goddess Dawn, God Agni, and the gods that wake in the morning and come in the morning, like the Açvins and others.

Every morning Agni is produced anew for the sacrifice; this secures for him the appropriate epithet "the youngest." On the other hand he is the same old Agni, and now comes a good deal of playful or mystic handling of this paradox. His new births are contrasted with his old; having grown old he is born again as a youth. Thus it happens that he is called "ancient" and "very young" in the same passage; the Vedic poets delight in this kind of mental see-saw. The mystery is shallow; what is meant is, that the vigorous life of the present-day Agni recalls his traditional importance in the past. There is no sacrificer older than Agni, for he conducted the first sacrifice. Just as he flames up to-

[1] Rig-Veda 10. 156. 4.
[2] Above, p. 73.

day at dawn so he shone forth under the auspices of former dawns at the sacrifice of many a great forefather: Bharata, or Vadhryaçva; Divodāsa, or Trasadasyu.

After having been kindled Agni is placed upon the altar or, if we trust the testimony of the ritual texts of the Veda, upon three altars.[1] Fagots are now piled on, fat oblations are poured in ; he waxes big; his tongues, three, or seven, shoot up ; he has four eyes, or a thousand eyes—both things mean that he is sharp-sighted ; his jaws are sharp; and his teeth shine golden, or his iron grinders clutch.   Then the figure is changed : he is flame-haired, tawny-haired, tawny-bearded; his glowing head faces in all directions. Ghee, or melted butter, is his food: he is therefore called ghee-backed, ghee-faced, ghee-haired. Once, even more boldly, Agni himself says, ghee is his eye. This is the point where Agni begins to take on a little more of the flesh and blood of personality upon the skeleton of his elemental qualities. For he receives the offerings neither passively nor selfishly.   At as late a time as that of the great Epic, the Mahābhārata[2] he is made to say : " The ghee that is poured into my mouth, in the way prescribed in the Veda, nourishes the Gods and the

---

[1] *Cf.* Rig-Veda 2. 36. 4 ; 5. 11. 2 ; 10. 105. 9.
   1. 7. 7. *ff* = 917 *ff.*

Manes . . . called by my mouth the Gods and the
Manes come to eat the ghee."

In fact the gods cannot subsist without him.   A
very neat story which, as usual, remains one of the
stock themes of story-telling India in later times,
tells in two hymns of the Rig-Veda[1] how Agni on
a certain occasion tired of this service. Agni has it
born in upon him that his older brothers have worn
themselves out in their job, and concludes that he
had better dodge a like fate.   Whereupon he escapes into the waters.   But the god Yama discovers
and betrays him, and Varuna, as the spokesman of
the gods, finally induces him for a consideration to
resume the task of expediting the sacrifice to the
gods.[2] The names which he obtains in this capacity,
such as "oblation-eater" and "oblation-carrier,"[3]
reappear familiarly in the Mahābhārata and later.
There they are pigeon-holed, along with numerous
other names, to be selected in the manner of the
Norse kennings, to vary the diction, to swell its
dignity, and to ease the task of the verse-maker.
With a different turn, he brings the gods to the sac-

[1] 10. 51 and 52.
[2] For other later tales of Agni lost and found again see the Mahābhārata legends in Holtzmann, *Agni nach den Vorstellungen des
Mahābhārata*, p. 12 *ff.*
[3] *Hutāça, hutāçana, hutabhuj, havyabhaksha,* etc.; *hutavaha, havy-
avah, havyavāhana,* etc.

rifice, and seats them on the strewn grass. He thus becomes familiar with the roads that connect heaven and earth, and becomes the regular messenger between the two. In this capacity he is associated with the Angiras, a race of mythic semi-divine priests whose name seems to be identical with Greek ἄγγελος (angel), "messenger." They also mediate between gods and men, and naturally Agni is an Angiras, the first seer Angiras, the ancient Angiras, the most inspired of the Angiras.

Agni officiates at the sacrifice and becomes the divine counterpart of the earthly priesthood: house-priest, serving-priest, and priest in general, as states the very first stanza of the Rig-Veda. As such he also inspires, or invents the brilliant speech and thought of prayer, and, what is very important, he frees from sin. For the sacrifice, of course, is the staple means of conciliating the gods when they are supposed to be angry. The idea of priesthood blends with that of seer and sage. He is so expert and well-travelled as to assume in a very pronounced sense the qualities of omniscience and omnipresence.[1]

He knows everything by virtue of his wisdom; he embraces wisdom as a felly does the wheel. The adjective *kavikratu*, "possessing the intellect of the

[1] *Cf.* Holtzmann's essay, cited above, p. 5.

sages," applies to him particularly, and the epithet
jātavedas, "having innate wisdom," is exclusively
his own.   From the function of archpriest and arch-
sage to godhead it is but a step.   Agni is the divine
benefactor of his worshipper who sweats to carry him
fuel: him he protects with a hundred iron walls, or
takes across all calamities, as in a ship over the sea.
And then, finally, he is divine monarch, surpassing
mighty heaven and all the worlds, is superior to all
the other gods who worship him, or takes his place
in the long line of supreme gods whom the poets
indifferently, or henotheistically, as Max Müller put
it, praise at convenient times with all the fervor
and all the resourceful verbiage which marks the
diction of the Rig-Veda:

> Then hail to Agni on his brilliant chariot,
> The shining signal of every holy sacrifice,
> Of every god in might divine the equal,
> The gracious guest of every pious mortal!

> Dressed out in all thy ornamented garments,
> Thou standest on the very navel of the earth,
> The hearth of sacrifice.   Born of the light,
> Both priest and king, shalt hither fetch th' immortals!

> For thou hast ever spread both earth and heaven,
> Tho' being their son thou hast spread out thy parents.
> Come hither, youthful god, to us that long for thee,
> And bring, O Son of Strength, the bright immortals!

> (Rig-Veda 10. 1. 5–7.)

I have followed the main current of Agni's life in
order to make clear the meaning of arrested personification, or arrested anthropomorphism. The Vedic
poets are far from restricting themselves to this one
view. Fire is not only in the sacral fire-sticks, but
he is visible everywhere: as sun and lightning in
the sky; as glint on the surface of the waters; as
the embryo of plants and trees that willingly give it
up when in flames; as the spark of flint and the
rocks; and even in the heat of the body, and as
vital force latent in all living things. Especially
remàrkable is the certainly Indo-European myth
which deals very clearly with a twin descent from
heaven: the descent of fire, and the descent of the
heavenly fluid. In its Vedic treatment the heavenly
fire is Agni of the lightning; the heavenly fluid is
soma, the ambrosial drink: " The one (namely, the
heavenly fire) Mātariçvan brought from heaven;
the other (namely, *soma*) the eagle brought from the
rock." [1] I have spoken before of the descent of the
heavenly fluid the descent of Agni from heaven is
doubtless connected with the lightning fire. Mātariçvan, however, who brings Agni, belongs to the
class of mythic persons for whom I have reserved
the attribute " opaque." Even this dramatic nature

[1] Rig-Veda, I. 93. 6.
[2] Above, p. 146.

act, which the plastic spirit of the Greeks shapes for
all time into the main motif of the Prometheus
tragedy, appears to the Vedic poets merely as
heaven's method of furnishing fire and *soma* for the
sacrifice: it does not turn into a real humanised
myth. And what I have deduced here in detail is
true of all of Agni's traits in the Veda; he is at one
moment element and phenomenon, at another person
and god, at all times as clear as his own light to
teach the nature of the gods.

I have used the term transparent in connection
with divine personifications whose naturalistic basis
and whose starting point in human consciousness is
absolutely clear. Now the term translucent, figure
of speech though it is, I wish to be understood in its
plain physical sense. It refers to mythic formations
whose structural outline may still be traced with a
great deal of truth, although it is obscured by incrus-
tations of secondary matter.   It is often merely the
loss of the original simple name which is the cause
of the obscuration. Divinities of the name "Dawn"
(Ushas), " Sun " (Sūrya), or " Fire " (Agni), bring
credentials that every one can read. But the quick
substitution of an attractive, or pointed epithet for
the original name may plague the investigator for all
time to come, and deprive him of mathematical certainty, even though every instinct draws him in the

right direction. An unusually unsympathetic sceptic
will not find it hard to rest his feet upon some pro-
jecting ledge of doubt, and all history cries out that
we must not try to dislodge sceptics by violence.
Every middle-aged student of Comparative Mythology and Comparative Philology recalls the time when
even the most complex myths were blandly explained as nature processes; nothing in that line
could be too fanciful and far-fetched to find adherents. No cock might crow in a fairy-tale without
becoming party to an involved and profound sun-
myth. We have all sobered much; there is now,
perhaps, too much insistence upon the element of
uncertainty which goes with the term ".probable,"
no matter how closely the probable may approach
certainty.

Tho two Açvins, the Dioscuri, are translucent
gods. They harbor some phenomenon of morning
light as one part of their dual character. The other
is probably the corresponding phenomenon at eve.
But just what this duality is we were unable to say.[1]
It is something to have limited this brilliant Indo-
European myth so far, and to find behind it reason
rather than idle fancy. The god Varuna, as we have
seen, belongs also to this class; for better or for
worse interpretation will turn to some phenomenon

[1] See above, p. 116.

of heaven which suggests the god's salient quality of overseer, be it encompassing sky, be it moon. I choose two other gods as the type of translucent gods, Vishnu and Pūshan ; in both cases we shall be engaged with variant aspects of the sun. This may seem to some minds a suspicious monotony of explanation, in fact it is the so-called solar theory. But I am nothing daunted : the sun is important and ever present with early observers ; I shall let him fight his own battles.

If I am not mistaken, I have done the cause of Vishnu a service in pointing out that the name itself is compounded of the two words *vi* and *snu*, meaning "through the back." [1] The leading fact in Vishnu's activity in the Veda is that he takes three strides (*tredhā vi kram*). A passage in the Sāma-Veda states that "Vishnu strode through over the back of the earth." [2] Here the word for "through" is *vi ;* the word for "back" is *sānu* (*snu*)—the two parts of the name Vishnu. The third of these enormous strides lands Vishnu in the highest heaven, in the bright realm of light, where even the winged birds do not dare to fly. [3] There in the highest stepping

---

[1] *American Journal of Philology*, vol. xvii., p. 428.

[2] Sāma-Veda 2. 1024, *yato vishnur vi cakrame pṛthivyā adhi sānavi*.

[3] Rig-Veda I. 155. 3, 5.

place is Vishnu's fount of honey.[1] This place is
identical with the highest place of Agni; Vishnu
guards the highest, or third place of Agni, the fire
on high, the sun.[2] There the gods and pious men
rejoice. Liberal sacrificers ever look forward to this
place; it is fixed like an eye in heaven.[3] Later Veda
texts clearly define the three steps as earth, atmosphere, and heaven. Vishnu represents the sun in
his ascent from the horizon of the earth, through
the atmosphere to the zenith, considered as the solar
paradise. His swift climb over the back of the universe through the cosmic triad justly arrested the
fancy of the poets, and they name him accordingly.
Instead of holding to the proper name of the sun, or
to his more familiar functions of giver of light and
life, they express in the name Vishnu, and in the
fancies connected with it the sufficiently remarkable
fact that his ascent from earth to the paradisiacal
zenith involves but three stations: earth, atmosphere, and heaven. From the earliest time Hindu
records show the greatest interest in this threefold
division of the universe.[4] Other notions, such as
that Vishnu marks off with his wide steps for his

[1] Rig-Veda I. 154. 5.
[2] *Ibid.*, 10. 1. 3.
[3] *Ibid.*, I. 22. 20.
[4] See above, p. 91.

worshippers corresponding breadth or wide scope for success and prosperity, and that he frees them from restraint and trouble, follow as an almost inevitable consequence. In a later time Vishnu is elevated to the highest place; he is one of the so-called Hindu Trinity. To the end he remains the Vishnu of the solar paradise to whom go the spirits of the departed pious. But at the same time he represents to his sectarian worshippers the pantheistic Brahma, or "all-soul," with which the soul of man is ultimately destined to unite.

I choose as the second example of a translucent god, the shepherd god Pūshan. His chief claim to usefulness is that he knows the roadways; protects from their dangers, such as wolves and robbers; guards cattle, so that they be not dashed to pieces in the ravine; brings them home unhurt when they have gone astray; and, in general, restores lost things. Pūshan personally drives the cows to pasture; he weaves the sheeps' dresses, and smoothes their coats; he carries a goad, and his car is drawn by goats. And seeing that he lives on mush or gruel, whereas the other gods revel in *soma* or ghee, his bucolic nature is pretty clear. His name means "Prospero," which may, of course, be the epithet of any benevolent god, and therefore veils rather than tells his particular character.

The following specimen shows the tone of the not too numerous hymns addressed to him:

Rig-Veda 6. 54.

Guide us, O Pūshan, to a man
Who, wise, straightway shall point the way,
And say to us : " Lo, here it is!"

With Pūshan joined let us go forth ;
He points our houses out to us,
And saith to us : " Right here they are !"

His chariot's wheel doth never break ;
Its seat doth never tumble down ;
Nor doth his wheel's rim ever crack.

Whoso payeth tribute to the god
Him Pūshan never doth forget ;
That man is first to gather wealth.

May Pūshan follow our kine,
May he protect our horses too,
And furnish us with solid wealth !

May naught be lost, nor aught be hurt ;
May naught be injured in the pit ;
Our cattle sound bring back to us !

May Pūshan pass his good right hand
Around about and far and wide,
And drive our lost goods back to us !

The standard interpretation of this god is again as a sun-god. This is well supported by some higher

mythic traits in which this god is not altogether
wanting. He is lord of all things that stand or
move ; almost the same words describe Sūrya (Helios).
He also is the lover or husband of the Sun-Maiden
Sūryā, that arch-flirt who carries on affairs with the
male Sūrya, the Açvins, and Soma. He alone has
the very ancient epithet *āghṛṇi* "glowing." This
fits the sun, and besides hardly any other article
than fire. Now fire Pūshan is not. To consider
him, under these circumstances, a mere "god Prospero," or an abstract "Lord of the Paths," is a good
deal like begging the question. Contrariwise his
abilities as path-finder, cattle god, and restorer of
lost things point to an overseeing heavenly body,
particularly if we may trust another Lithuanian folk-
song (*daina*) which I may be permitted to quote :

> Oh, at the yester even tide
> I lost my little lamb !
> Oh, who shall help me go and seek
> My only little lamb ?

> I went and asked the morning star,
> The morning star replied :
> " I have to build the dear sun's fire
> At morrow's morning tide."

> I went and asked the evening star,
> The evening star replied :
> " I have to make the dear sun's bed
> At every even tide."

I went and asked the waning moon,
The waning moon replied :
" I have been smitten with a sword,[1]
My sorry face I hide."

I went and asked the lovely sun,
The dear sun gave reply ;
" Nine days I 'll seek, and on the tenth
I 'll not set in the sky."[2]

The familiar notion that the sun oversees every-thing[3] appeals in this instance to the simple reasoning power of shepherd folk.　A more suitable origin for a shepherd god it is not easy to imagine.　They there-fore dress him out in shepherd's clothes, feed him on shepherd's food, and turn him into a heavenly bell-wether of their flocks.　But his real natural history does not seem to me to be very much disguised by the simple-minded fable.　We may safely call Pūshan a translucent god.

The most prominent of the gods of the Rig-Veda is Indra.　About two hundred and fifty hymns are devoted to his praise, perhaps one-fourth of all the hymns of the collection.　No account of Vedic religion can pass by his big personality, and yet his essence and quality are that of lower, rather than higher

---

[1] *Cf.* the Lithuanian folk-song, above, p. 114.

[2] Professor Chase's rendering, *Transactions of the American Philo-logical Association*, vol. xxxi., p. 193.

[3] Ἥλιος πανόπτης, *Iliad* 3. 277 ; Æschylus, *Prometheus Bound*, 91.

religious conceptions, even if we adopt no higher standard than the Rig-Veda. To the growingly finer religious thought of the later Veda Indra contributes nothing positive. Negatively, the coarse grain and the fleshliness of his character which, taken all in all, are foreign to the gods of the Vedic Pantheon, arrest very unfavorable attention. Indra is so grossly anthropomorphic, that is, he embodies so completely the human qualities of brag and bluster, gluttony, drunkenness, and lust, as to make him the peg upon which to hang scepticism. In that way he contributes negatively to the advance of Hindu thought. Of this later on.

This god has remained opaque to the eye of Vedic study. He is not wanting in superlative cosmic qualities. In fact the poets never, unless except perhaps in the case of Varuna, come nearer biting off more than they can chew, than when engaged in lauding Indra. He has no counterpart among those born or to be born. No one, celestial or terrestrial, has been born, or shall be born, like unto him. All the gods yield to him in might and strength.[1] He supports earth and sky, or spreads out the earth.[2] More particularly, he is the Hindu Hercules and demiurge[4] the doer of great deeds for the people.

[1] Rig-Veda 4. 18. 4; 7. 32. 2; 8. 51. 7.
[2] *Ibid.*, 2. 15. 2.

He slays dragons and monsters; he is the typical slayer of the foes of the pious sacrificer. To these deeds of heroic valor he is stimulated by immense potations of intoxicating *soma*. In order to accomplish the slaughter of the arch-dragon Vritra he drank on one occasion three lakes of that delightful beverage, so that decidedly he had a jag on, which, it has been noted, rhymes well with dragon. Accordingly he has a tremendous body, strong jaws and lips. He is tawny-haired and bearded, carries a club in his hand, and fights on a chariot drawn by two bay steeds. In general the Vedic poets cannot be accused of coarseness; yet it seems that, in this instance, they were irresistibly attracted by the mighty deeds of this, "Lord of Strength," as they call him. This is probably owing to the fact that he is felt to be the national hero of the Aryan invaders in their struggles against the dark-skinned aborigines, whom they must overcome in order to hold possession of the land which they invaded. And nations are never coarser than when they put their own nationality into antagonism against another nation. In a recent war, familiar to all of us, a prominent warrior on the side of the stronger nation expressed his consuming desire to make, by his own valorous deeds, the language of the weaker nation the vernacular of Hades. This is the spirit of the worship of Indra.

But it would be a mistake to suppose that Indra is a mere coarse embodiment of the jingo valor of a superior race exercised against a weak enemy fated to subjection. Indra's character is not even translucent, that is, we can no longer define his origin with certainty, but there is no doubt that he originated somewhere in visible nature. The difficulty is to tell where. To begin with, there is no belittling the fact that Indra's origin is prehistoric. His name occurs in the Avesta (Andra) where, as is often the case with earlier Aryan divinities, he is degraded to a demon. But his chief Vedic epithet, Vritrahan, " Slayer of Vritra," is the same name as that of the abstract genius of Victory, Verethraghna in the Avesta, and the Armenian dragon slayer Vahagn.[1]   On the other hand there is no real Indra literature outside of India. If then we are forced to turn to India in order to explain Indra, we must not forget that his origin is outside of India and precedes Hindu history.

The following specimen, Rig-Veda i. 32, is done into prose, rather than into metre, in order to show clearly how Indra and his principal exploit, namely, the slaughter of the dragon Vritra and the liberation of the waters, really presents itself to the mind of the poets:

[1] See Hillebrandt, *Vedische Mythologie*, vol. iii., p. 188 *ff.*

1. Let me now tell forth the heroic deeds of Indra, which he that wields the club performed of yore. He slew the dragon, broke the way for the waters ; he cleft the belly of the mountains.

2. He slew the dragon who lay upon the mountain. God Tvashtar forged for him his heavenly club. Like roaring cattle, down came the waters, flowing swiftly to the sea.

3. Lusty as a bull, Indra demanded soma ; from three vats drank he of the pressed drink. His missile bolt he took in hand, the generous god, and slew the first-born of the dragons.

4. When thou didst smite, O Indra, the first-born of the dragons, when thou didst make naught of the wiles of the wily, then, bringing out both sun and heaven and dawn, thou verily didst not find a foeman worthy of thy steel.

6. A drunken weakling, Vritra, did challenge the great hero, the mighty, dashing fighter. He did not withstand the impact of his weapons : with broken nose lay shattered he whose foe was Indra.

7. Over him lying so, like a broken reed, the waters go flowing at will. Those (very waters) which Vritra had encompassed with his might, at the feet of them the dragon prone lay stretched.

13. Nor thunder, nor lightning did help him ; nor the hail-storm which he cast about him. When Indra and the dragon fought their battle, then even for future times the liberal god won the battle.

These stanzas carry us into the very midst of a

12

myth whose three elements bring with them three questions: First, what are the waters? Secondly, who is Vritra that shuts them in? Thirdly, who is Indra that liberates them after a struggle that puts him so very much on his mettle? Hindu tradition, commentators and later classical Sanskrit literature, has always had an unhesitating answer: The waters are rain; Vritra is the cloud that shuts them off from the earth; Indra, therefore, is the storm or thunder god that rends the clouds with his lightning bolt and frees their waters. This interpretation, at first sight thoroughly sensible and most satisfactorily suggestive, was for a good while held to be good by most western students of the Veda and Comparative Mythology. The trouble with it turned out to be that the Veda has the real storm and rain god Parjanya,[1] and that the hymns addressed to him describe thunder-storms in language that is very different, and cannot be mistaken for anything else than the phenomena of the thunder-storm. The sober facts of the Indra-Vritra myth are as follows: A god armed with a bolt fights a dragon or serpent who holds the rivers in confinement within the mountains. He kills the dragon, cleaves the mountains. The rivers flow from the mountains to the sea. Thus the texts: there is nothing to show that

[1] See above, p. 111.

the mountains mean clouds, and the rivers the flow of rain.

After such and other premonitory symptoms of scepticism and unrest, Professor Hillebrandt has recently advanced a new theory of Indra, Vritra, and the waters, which he expounds with great ingenuity and learning.[1] He argues that the streams of India and the neighboring Iranian countries are at their lowest level in the winter; that the confiner of their waters is the frozen winter, conceived as a winter monster by the name of Vritra, "confiner;" that Vritra holds captive the rivers on the heights of the glacier mountains; and that, consequently, Indra can be no other than the spring or summer sun who frees them from the clutches of the winter dragon: " Behold, in winter's chain sleeps the song of the waterfall under the dungeon roof of crystal ice!" So sings a Swedish poet, Count Snoiisky. And another Swedish poet, Andreas Aabel, rings out the antistrophe: " Hear the mountains proud cascade! Just now it has broken winter's check and prison, and now it courses free along its road!"[2]

Now it is true that the emergence of spring from winter is sometimes treated poetically as a battle. We can understand this much better in a north coun-

[1] See Hillebrandt, *Vedische Mythologie*, vol. iii., p. 157 *ff*.
[2] See *ibid*, p. 187.

try like Sweden where the conflict is hard and long. Even there these phenomena seem hardly to suggest so fierce and Herculean a contest as that which is supposed to take place between Indra and the frost giant Vritra:

Released from ice are stream and brook,
By spring-tide's enchanting, enlivening look.

These words of Goethe seem to come so much nearer to what might be expected.

But over and beyond, Indra performs in his professional capacity of Hercules a large assortment of other " stunts." He releases the cows from the stables of the avaricious who confine them and will not sacrifice them to the gods. He also performs the heavenly analogue of this deed: he breaks open the stables of darkness, presided over by another demon of the name of Vala, and releases the heavenly cows, that is, the light of dawn and the sun. It seems impossible to hold aloof this important myth from the classical myths of Heracles and three-headed Geryon, and Hercules and three-headed Cacus. Hercules carries off the cattle which belong to the monster, or, in the case of Cacus, which the monster had stolen from the hero, and had hidden away in his cave.[1] Indra, moreover, kills a great variety of other demons. To the immediate con-

[1] See Oldenberg, *Die Religion des Veda*, p. 143 *ff*.

ception of the Veda he is indeed a sort of Hercules, the most personal of all the gods, so personal that people begin to doubt his existence, and ask, " Who has seen him?"   I have brought much sympathy to Professor Hillebrandt's interpretation which I hope may in the end turn out to be the right one ; for the present it has left me in the frame of mind indicated by the word opaque.   I confess, I cannot pass over as lightly as does Hillebrandt the unanimous Hindu tradition that Vritra is the cloud.   The partnership of Indra with Vāyu " Wind " is paralleled suggestively by the association of Parjanya and Vāta, " Wind." Parjanya is beyond peradventure a god of the thunder-storm.   It is therefore still possible that the myth of Indra, Vritra, and the waters represents a specialised poetic treatment of a myth of thunderstorm, cloud, and rain.   The myth may have, so to speak, been brought down to earth: Indra, the storm god, becomes a Hercules, and kills a dragon who hoards in the mountains (formerly, the clouds), the rivers (formerly, the rain of the clouds).   For a final solution of this most important theme in mythology it seems to me that we must look to the future.   The confirmation of Hillebrandt's masterly theory, if it comes at all, must come from Iran or Western Asia.   Such confirmation should establish more definitely Indra's and Vritra's character in the

Indo-Persian time from which, if not from a still
earlier time, dates their beginning. If these earlier
data should by any chance ever show Indra and
Vritra in the mutual relation of summer and winter,
then Hillebrandt's hypothesis, and I fear not until
then, would be triumphantly vindicated.

RELIGIOUS CONCEPTIONS AND RELIGIOUS FEELING
IN THE VEDA.

The religion of the Rig-Veda, as we have seen,
is in its most superficial aspect a priestly religion
of works designed to propitiate and to barter with
personal gods. The outer form in which it presents itself is as poetry of the sacrifice. The sacrifice with its ceremonial formalities is, as I have
ventured to say, the epidermis of Vedic religion.
In its next layer the religion of the Veda is expressed in hymnal worship of the same personal
gods who get the offerings. Whatever we may say
about the origin of these gods, one by one, they are
to the Hindu conception for the most part related to
the visible and audible forces of nature. Nature in
its larger aspect, cosmic nature, is the prime source
of inspiration of the Vedic religious bard, just as it
was the inspiration of his prehistoric Aryan and Indo-
European ancestors. The conception of nature and
the nature gods, notwithstanding many crudities, is

singularly poetic.   I shall show later that the religious consciousness, in so far as it concentrates itself
upon their admiration and praise, marks in fact the
highest point in the Vedic Rishis' mental and spiritual possibilities.   In the end it will be found to be
something more than religious poetry ; it is rather
religion or religious sense expressing itself as poetic
inspiration.   Anyhow we must not believe that the
ritual has swamped everything.   The delight in the
gods, especially the half-personalised nature forces
which are treated as gods, is too unstinted and generous to allow us to doubt its genuineness.   I am
sure that many, if not all, of these poets addressed
their beautiful hymns to the goddess Dawn, or to
the sun-god Sūrya with the full swing of creative
poets, delighting in their theme for the theme's sake,
and chiseling their poems for the poems' sake.   We
may believe that these priest-poets at times, when
in their best vein, asked the favor of the gods not
as greedy beggars, but as joyously unconscious bene-
ficiaries of divinities whose power to reward is incidental to their inherent generous nature, and who,
therefore present themselves as a brilliant and worthy
theme of song.

But the every-day existence of these men is
something different.   It is loaded down with those
dreadful practicalities.   They must live by this

very trade of theirs, namely, praise of the gods
and purveyance of the sacrifice. When they turn
their minds away, as they constantly do and must do,
from those well-conceived personifications they tend
downward. As middle-men between the gods and
men they must, above all, take care of men, their
own selves not least of all. Men can subsist and
prosper only if the gods return in kind. The gods,
on the whole, are good ; they do not beat down the
requests of him that comes with prayer and cup of
soma. Reciprocity, frank unconditional reciprocity,
thus becomes an accepted motive : " Give thou to
me, I give to thee," is the formula.[1] The sacrificing
king, or rich householder, is thereby placed between
the upper and the nether mill-stone : he must satisfy
both gods and priests, each of whom show a surprising habit of becoming more and more exacting
as time goes by. In this way the high poetic quality
of Vedic religion is crowded and choked by many
conceptions mean from the start, or bent by these
circumstances into a mean shape. The gods themselves, notwithstanding their luminous origin, are
brought down to the plane of human weakness.
Open to adulation, they become vain ; eager for advantage, they become shifty; reflecting human desires,
they become sordid, and in some cases even indecent.

[1] *dehi me dadāmi te.*   Cf. the Roman *do ut des.*

In the first place, Vedic poets engage in a sort of scramble for the gods. The gods cannot be in one and the same place at the same time, and cannot grant all the conflicting wishes of their numerous suppliants. I have dealt with this theme which may interest the broader students of the history of religions, in a recent paper presented to the XIVth International Congress of Orientalists, held at Algiers in 1905.[1] The title of the paper, *On Conflicting Prayers and Sacrifices*, tells a good deal of the story. The notion which comes out quite persistently is that it requires art to "hog" the gods, and it is not a very delectable notion either from the æsthetic or the ethical point of view. Yet not less so perhaps than the *Te Deum laudamus* over the slaughter of enemies, which has been known to be chanted by both sides at the same time when each side claimed victory.[2]

[1] See *Johns Hopkins University Circulars* of 1906, Nr. 10, p. 1 *ff*.
[2] Or consider :

> " Gieb regen und gieb sonnenschein
>   Für Reuss und Schleuss und Lobenstein ;
>   Und wollen andre auch was ha'n
>   So mögen sie's dir selber sa'n."

My colleague, Professor Gildersleeve, proposes the following English transfusion :

> " Give rain and sunshine we implo'
>   For us upon the Eastern sho' ;
>   If any others want a share
>   Themselves may offer up the prayer."

So, for instance, poets of the ancient family of bards, the Vasishthas, on a certain occasion brag that they made Indra prefer their own *soma* libations to those of Pāçadyumna Vāyata, though the latter had gone to the trouble of fetching Indra from a great distance.   Frantically emphatic prayer; imprecation of the man who is praying at the same time; and naughty tricks of various sorts show us under this aspect the whole world of praying and sacrificing men engaged in a sort of universal game of tag: the hindmost is "it."   The Vedic Hindus have made a sad botch of this matter.   I am glad to say that this particular crudity passes out at the end of the Vedic period with the slow "twilight of the gods" which shifts the interest from polytheism, myth, and sacrifice to the theosophic speculations of the Upanishads. When the personal gods emerge again in later Hinduism, they are much clarified; at least the risky question about their presence in many places at one and the same time, and the equitable distribution of their favors is, as far as I know, never asked again.

There is scarcely any idea which has suffered so much from the utilitarian aspects of Vedic religion as the Vedic idea of faith.   To begin with, the word itself is of interest; it is *çraddhā*, the sound for sound equivalent of Latin and our own *credo*.   The etymological meaning of this word is absolutely

transparent. It means "to set one's heart upon."
This etymology, which is still quite clear to the Vedic poets, shows it full of ethical possibilities. The
word starts well in the Rig-Veda. It means first of
all belief in the existence and godhead of the gods.
So, a poet is anxious to make certain the position of
the god Indra, that blustering, pinchbeck, braggart,
Herculean god whose shortcomings have gone far to
establish a certain position for the Vedic freethinker.
The poets say of him :

"The terrible one of whom they ask, where is he?
Nay verily they say of him, he is not at all. He makes
shrink the goods of his enemy like a gambler the stakes
of his opponent : Put your faith in him—He, O folks, is
Indra."

(Rig-Veda 2. 12. 5.)

"As a strong warrior, he verily fights with might
great battles in behalf of the people. Aye, then they have
faith in strong Indra, as he hurls down his weapon."

(Rig-Veda 1. 55, 5.)

"Who, what mortal, can overcome him whose treasure
thou art, O Indra? Through faith in thee, O liberal
God, on the decisive day, does he that strives obtain
booty."

(Rig-Veda 7. 32. 14.)

So there is no doubt that faith means the belief in
the existence of the gods, and their interference in
the life of man. It would be doing injustice to those

early believers to say that they did not develop the
idea beyond this stage of mere primary utility. A
later text of the Yajur-Veda says : Faith is truth,
and unfaith is lies :

"The creator (Prajāpati) having beheld two qualities
separated truth and lie from one another. He put unfaith into lie, faith he placed into truth."
(Vājasaneyi Samhitā 19. 77)

Next, faith is wisdom ; faith is the sister of wisdom:
The fool saith in his heart, " there is no god."   In
order to disprove his folly it becomes needful to
couple the ideas of Faith and Wisdom.   From a later
time we have very interesting accounts of the initia-
tion of disciples, and their instruction in the Vedas.
Teacher and pupil in a kind of dramatic dialogue carry
on the solemn action : " Teach me the revealed books
(of the Veda), my Lord !" saith the pupil.   " I teach
thee the revealed books," replieth the teacher.
" Teach me the Vedic tradition, my Lord!" saith the
pupil.   " I teach thee the Vedic tradition," replieth
the teacher.   " Teach me Faith and Wisdom, my
Lord!" saith the pupil.   " I teach thee Faith and
Wisdom." [1] In another text, as the pupil puts on the
sacred girdle which he wears during disciplehood, he
addresses it :

[1] See Çānkhāyana **Grihyasūtra** 2. 7, and compare Āçvalāyana
Grihyasūtra 3. 9. 1.

" Daughter of Faith, born of Zeal, sister was she of the Seers that did create the beings.   Do thou, O girdle, assign to us Thought and Wisdom ; also assign to us Zeal and Strength."

(Atharva-Veda 6. 133. 4.)

Faith kindles the sacrifice-fire and, by way of return, the sacred fire, this chief emblem of Brahmanical religion, is in charge of both Faith and Wisdom :

> " Through Faith the fire is kindled,
> Through Faith the oblation is offered.
> Faith, that stands at the head of fortune,
> Her do we with our song proclaim."

(Rig-Veda 10. 151. 1.)

On the other hand, the Brahmanical disciple appeals to Agni Jātavedas (the holy fire) to preserve for him faith and wisdom, to keep intact his memory, so that he may not forget the sacred texts, and to secure him in well-being.[1]

Next, Faith becomes a person, a goddess.   That would not be bad but for the mechanical character which she then assumes.   Imagine—and in order to imagine this one must be pretty well steeped in Hinduism—the frame of mind of a poet who skilfully exalts the goddess Faith, but finally asks her to accept oblations :

---

[1] Çānkhāyana Grihyasūtra 2. 10. 6.

" Through Faith the gods obtain their divine quality;
  Faith, the goddess, is the foundation of the world.
  May she pleased come to our sacrifice,
  Bring our wish as her child, and grant us immortality!

" Faith, the goddess, is the first-born of divine order,
  Upholder of all, foundation of the world,
  That Faith do we revere with our oblations;
  May she create for us an immortal world."
                    (Taittirīya Brāhmana 3. 12. 3. 1, 2.)

" Faith dwells within the gods,
  Faith dwells upon this world,
  Faith, the mother of wishes—
  With oblations do we prosper her."
                    (Taittirīya Brāhmana 2. 8. 8).

So far so good. All that is still a development of
the idea of faith in harmony with a decent belief in
personal gods. Unfortunately, the Vedic conception
of faith, at least the prominent or average conception
sinks to a much lower plane. In the main and in the
end, faith expresses itself in works, and the Brahmans
who are anything but mealy-mouthed have seen to
it that they shall be benefited by these works. In
other words, he who gives baksheesh (*dakshinā*) to
the Brahmans, he has faith (*çraddhā*). In a hymn that
is otherwise not badly pitched the poet requests the
personified goddess Faith to make his poetic work
take well with the liberal sacrificer, and to make him

persona grata "with him that giveth, and him that shall give."[1] An exceedingly interesting hymn of the Atharva-Veda, not at all wanting in poetic inspiration, is addressed to the demoness "Grudge," or "Avarice." The name of the lady is Arāti. Of course she is primarily an abstraction. Yet she appears as a full-fledged person: she has a golden complexion, is lovely, rests upon golden cushions; is in fact quite an Apsaras, or "schoene Teufelinne," as the old German poetry has it in for Venus. With all her charms she is coaxed to go away:

"Bring (wealth) to us, do not stand in our way, O Arāti; do not keep from us the sacrificial fee when it is being taken to us! Homage be to the power of grudge, to the power of baffling! Adoration to Arāti!

"Him whom I implore with holy word (Vāc Sarasvatī), the yoke-fellow of thought, may Faith enter him to-day, aroused by the burnished *soma* drink!"

(Atharva-Veda 5. 7. 1, 5.)

That is to say, when the burnished *soma* drink sparkles in the cup, when the pious emotion that comes from the skilful hymn stirs the heart of the rich sacrificer, then enters into him Faith. But what kind? The kind that drives out niggardliness. Then he gives to the Brahmans. How the Brahmans do long for baksheesh, especially when they are poor!

[1] Rig-Veda 10. 151. 2, 3.

There is the record of one who plaintively ejac-
ulates: "What gentleman, desirous of more possessions will get us out of this wretched misery?
Who desireth to sacrifice, and who is willing to
give presents? Who desireth long life from the
gods?"[1]

Even this mean and selfish construction of Faith,
on one famous occasion at least turns forth a better
side. A zealous young Brahman, Naciketas by name,
observes that baksheesh is by way of being freely
given. In fact his father Vājaçravasa has performed
a desperately pious sacrifice, the "All-his-property-
sacrifice"—luscious morsel for the Brahmans. He
has given away in sacrifice and attendant fees all
that he possesses. Then Faith enters into the boy
Naciketas. He wishes, so to say, "to get into the
band-wagon." He startles his father by asking: "To
whom wilt thou give me?" The father replies: "To
death"—we can imagine the formula that would
come from the lips of a modern fond father, if his
son were to ask him a question so very awkward.
Naciketas takes him literally and goes down to
Yama, the God of Death. He manages, however, to
get the better of Yama, not only enjoying his
hospitality, but also extracting from him certain

[1] Atharva-Veda 7. 103. 1. *Cf.* Ludwig, *Der Rig-Veda*, vol. iii., p.
283 *ff*; the author, *American Journal of Philology*, vol. xvii, p. 408 *ff*.

profound information concerning the riddle of existence.[1]

Now I shall not claim that this important concept was unmixedly mean and unspiritual. Indeed we have seen that it is not wholly so. This much, however, is clear that the anxious mind of the ritual is almost entirely fastened upon Faith as the promoter of the sacrifice and its attendant gifts to the Brahmans. In the end *açraddha*, " devoid of faith," is the typical epithet of the demons of avarice, the Panis, who withhold the cows from the gods and the Brahmans. One or two writers have the hardihood to put up a chain of four links: Faith, Consecration, Sacrifice, Baksheesh.[2] Since consecration (*dīkshā*) in this connection means really nothing but ancient hocus-pocus preliminary to the sacrifice, where, we may ask, is there a franker avowal of shady motives that ordinarily present themselves elsewhere with a thick coat of whitewash ?

But what is there in it for the sacrificer, we may ask ? It is all very well for him to silence those raucous voices of demand, and keep giving—for a while. He must in the long run get something in return, or he will balk. Our texts, explicit if nothing else, leave no doubt in our minds as to the way in which

[1] See the first book of the Katha Upanishad.
[2] Atharva-Veda 15. 16. 4. *ff.* ; Gopatha Brāhmana I. 1.39.

13

the sacrificer was rewarded, or thought he was rewarded, under this otherwise monotonously one-
sided arrangement.   We have seen that Faith,
Çraddhā, is personified.   Now the sacrifice, called
ishṭa, and the baksheesh, called (by another name)
pūrta, enter into a close compound, the *ishṭāpūrta*.
They, in their turn, get to have a kind of personal
reality, and turn into a kind of beneficent genius, or
perhaps better a kind of solid asset which becomes
useful with the gods during life, and, mark you, after
death as well.   During life, the god helps him who
sacrifices and gives baksheesh ; he adds to, does not
rob his property.[1]   But it is for the most part a
question of future reward.   In a well-known funeral
hymn of the Rig-Veda the corpse is addressed most
realistically :

" Do thou join the Fathers, do thou join Yama, join
thy *ishṭāpūrta* (that which thou hast sacrificed and
given to the priests) in the highest heaven ! "

(Rig-Veda 10. 14. 8.)

And the following is a particularly realistic treatment of the same ideas.   Again a dead man is
blessed as he goes to heaven :

" Know him (the pious dead), O ye associated gods in
the highest heaven, recognise his form !   When he shall
have arrived by the paths that lead to the gods, disclose

[1] Rig-Veda 6. 28. 2.

to him his *ishṭāpūrta* (that is, the merit which he has
accumulated through sacrifice and liberality to the
priests) ! "

(Taittirīya Samhitā 5. 7. 7. 1.)

And so another poet, in a better vein, says in a
verse that has become famous in India :

" The highest step of Vishnu (that is the solar paradise) is ever seen by the liberal giver : it is fixed like an
eye in the heavens."

(Rig-Veda 1. 22. 20.)

At a later time when the Hindus in their highest
mood turn the ordinary gods into supernumeraries,
when metempsychosis takes the place of a journey
to heaven, when they have sloughed off priests, sacrifice fire, spoon, and ghee, all that is changed.   The
degraded Çraddhā or Faith is replaced by Bhakti,
" Devotion," that is, devotion to the Eternal True,
Only Being that is at the root of all things.   The
ishṭāpūrta, piled up in the savings-bank of heaven,
where Yama and the Fathers are engaged in everlasting feasts, is replaced by *karma*, the accumulated
deeds of a given lifetime and the attendant evolution
which these deeds have worked upon the spirit.
This so definitely shapes character as to determine
the nature of the next rebirth, until a perfect life
shall free the mortal from the toils of all existence,

and replace him in the bosom of the One True Being. Of all this later on.

However, even these saccharine promises about the accumulated credit given in heaven for sacrifice and baksheesh seem not to have been regarded by the poet priests as a sufficient guarantee that they might securely count upon that faith which meant works useful to them. They employ another device. Being skilled verse-smiths, they begin to use their craft to forge chains of poetry which shall hold rich patrons willing captives. They compose the so-called *dāna-stutis*, "gift-praises," or *gāthā nāraçaṅsyaḥ*, "stanzas singing the praise of men."[1] In dithyrambic language exorbitant gifts on the part of generous givers of old, mythic kings and patrons, are narrated, so as to stimulate the potential patron of the present day. They sing these praises so stridently that the Vedic texts themselves, in their soberer moments, decry the "gift-praises" as lies and pollution. The poet of a "stanza singing the praise of men" and the brandy-drunkard are likened unto one another: they are polluted, their gifts must not be accepted. I question whether the religious literature of any other people contains anything that resembles either in character or extent the "gift-

[1] *Cf*. Ludwig, *Der Rig-Veda*, vol. iii., p. 274 *ff.;* Bloomfield, *The Atharva-Veda* (*Indo-Aryan Encyclopædia*), p. 100.

praises" of the Veda ; the type is thoroughly Hindu in its naïveté and its boundlessness.

To begin with, there is in the Rig-Veda a doubtless late hymn consecrated to Dakshinā, or "Baksheesh." It is only a poetaster who undertakes, as he says, to unfold "the broad road of Baksheesh," *i. e.* to show how important it is to keep giving. Then, with refreshing obviousness he claims :

"Those that give *dakshinā* dwell on high in the heavens ; they that give horses dwell with the sun. They that give gold partake of immortality ; and they that give garments, O Soma, prolong their lives."

(Rig-Veda 10. 107. 2.)

There are forty or more " gift-praises " in the Rig-Veda alone ; they continue throughout the rest of the Veda. I do not mean to dwell upon them beyond a single example. We may remark, however, that some of this baksheesh must have proved a veritable elephant on the hands of the receiver, except for the fact that it was as a rule imaginary baksheesh :

"Listen, ye folks, to this : (a song) in praise of a hero shall be sung ! Six thousand and ninety cows did we get (when we were) with Kauruma among the Ruçamas !

"Kauruma presented the Seer with a hundred jewels, ten chaplets, three hundred steeds, and ten thousand cattle."

(Atharva-Veda 20. 127. 1, 3.)

Operations on such a scale are calculated to show the magnates of the present day meat-packing trust that they have yet to learn from these arch-flatterers a trick or two in the way of collecting cattle.

If my hearers shall ask now what, after all this, is the essence of Rig-Vedic religion, I am for my part not unready to answer in accordance with hints thrown out before. It is poetry, or rather, more precisely, poetic exaltation, or the pride and joy of poetic creativeness. This is at first conceived to be favored and promoted by the gods, because they get the fruit of it in the form of praise and flattery. The finer the frenzy of the poet and the more finished the product of his art, the better pleased are the gods. Therefore the gods, next, co-operate with the poets, promoting their devotion and its expression. Finally, these twin factors of devoted fervor and its successful utterance in hymns and stanzas create sensations of satisfaction which are easily taken for sanctification. At first the article is not very genuine. But it goes on being the receptacle of better thoughts until it grows into what we may consider real religious feeling.

To some extent we can test this statement by showing what the religious feeling of the Veda is not, rather than what it is. The frank system of barter of the sacrificer's *soma* and ghee for the god's good gift and protection, with considerably more than one-eighth of one per cent. brokerage for the priest—that, surely, is not the religious feeling in the souls of the composers of the Rig-Veda hymns. I have taken pains to show how constantly present is this external side of their religion : may the religion that is free from all external considerations, the religion from which is absent every form of safe-guarding self, throw the first stone.

The contemplation of the glory of the gods as a matter of intellectual wonder is expressed times without end.   It does not seem to me to have quite the true ring.   It is perfunctory ; it is told by rote. God after god steps into line and gets it.   They each in turn establish the heavens and the earth ; they start the sun on his course, almost indifferently well. Perhaps, as I have hinted before, their rotation in the ritual, rather than forgetfulness of the virtues of the preceding god, is the truth at the bottom of this kathenotheism or henotheism, as Max Müller called it.   It is polytheism grown cold in service, and unnice in its distinctions, leading to an opportunist monotheism in which every god takes hold of the sceptre and none keeps it.   Anyhow it is very mechanical.   No one who reads in the hymns the endless accounts of the wonderful performances of the gods will deny that the poets at times grow truly warm and feel their theme. Sometimes they are really carried away by it. But I do not believe that either the greatness and majesty, or the incomprehensibleness of the gods, have produced a permanent impression of their superiority and perfection which should permit us to speak of settled intellectual religious consciousness in the Rig-Veda.

Most conspicuously there is no sentimental relation of any great depth between gods and men, and therefore no piety in the higher sense of the word. I mean piety that is not mere emotional self-excitement, but reasonable and settled reverence of tried and true gods. As a matter of fact the gods are good, and, at least in a general way, they are just also. In India, as we have seen, the gods have in charge especially the order of the world, and that is at the proper time, to the advantage of the suppliant mortal. Conversely, and especially, god Varuna stands ready to punish the wrong-doer. The poets sometimes describe Varuna's power, and the sense of their own unworthiness or sinfulness in language that reminds us of the Psalmist. Varuna, however, is no longer pre-eminent even in the Rig-Veda: he has left no really lasting impression on India's religions. If Varuna had prevailed India would have become monotheistic and theocratic, which it never did.

Occasionally a start is made towards a warmly glowing relation of love and confidence ; the singer in need of help trusts that the god will help him. But there is no permanent, clarified, unselfish love of the gods such as overrides the experience of their instability, such as lives down the melancholy fact that they do not always help.   And we have seen what faith is in the Veda : it is the faith that manifests itself in works.   The Vedic poets are trained "master-singers." Such poets are not likely to penetrate far into the soul of man.   There is no real warmth or depth, no passionate indistinct feeling, no unsatisfied longing which can be made hopefully endurable, or even pleasurable and exalting, through the mystery of a relationship with perfect beings, understood by each individual soul in its own way. Anything like a contemplative, trustful joy in the perfection of the gods comes much later : it is of the Bhagavadgītā, rather than the Rig-Veda.

But these master-singers do believe in their own art ; in their wonderful poetry, and in the exaltation of mind which goes with its composition. The gods accept both the poetry and the devout mind at the value put upon them by the poets ; the poets are serenely certain that the gods are well satisfied.[1]   This

---

[1] " Like (a cow) her calf so do the poets lick (the gods) with their prayers," says Rig-Veda 10. 123. 1.

then is the state of mind that approaches genuine
and lasting religious feeling in the Rig-Veda:
belief in the beauty and fitness of those glittering, rhythmical, and assonant stanzas; genuine
rapture over the excited, throbbing mind, while
the glow of composition is upon the poet. The
poet calls himself *vipra*, "inspired"; calls his
compositions *vipah*, "inspirations"; and when he
composes, *vepate matī*, "he is inspired in his mind."
In the poet's pride of exquisite workmanship and the
gods' unresisting admiration, the Rig-Veda makes
us forget at times that unpleasant economic foundation of the performance, namely flattery and cajolery of the gods—for what there is in it.[1] Soon both
gods and men are engaged fraternally in promoting
devotion and its best possible expression in hymns,
as things of intrinsic worth, as beautiful elevated
cosmic potencies. And so we finally find at the
summit of this thought, the captivating and impor
tant prayer of the poet of the Sāvitrī stanza,[2] that
the god himself shall inspire his devotion.

I have used the word "master-singers." We may
take this word quite stringently and seriously. The
hymns often allude to the songs of old that were com-

[1] Rig-Veda 8. 21. 6 puts this baldly to god Indra: "We cite you
hither with this prayer; don't bethink yourself a minute. We have
wishes, you have gifts. Here we are with our songs."

[2] See above p 86.

posed by the Rishis of the past. The very first
hymn in the Rig-Veda strikes this note in its second
stanza : " Agni, worthy to be adored by the ancient
Rishis and the present ones—may he conduct the
gods hither ! " Another time a poet of the family of
Kanva sings [1] : " In the spirit of the olden times do I
dress out my songs like (the poet) Kanva, through
which (god) Indra gets his fiery strength."   Or again:
" (Hear), O Indra, him that hath produced for thee a
new and lovely song, with comprehending mind a
pious song such as of yore has strengthened the divine order of the universe."[2] In more confident or
ecstatic temper, the poets often declare that they
have produced new songs of praise, and that, in their
opinion, these are first-rate songs. One poet recom-
mends his " new, beautiful song of praise, that comes
from the heart;" another exclaims : " I bring forward
my word, the new, the fresh-born." With all due
respect to their predecessors this pretty nearly
amounts to saying that the new hymns are just as
good as the old, in addition to having the charm of
novelty. One thing is certain : we have nothing
like beginnings before us. The Rig-Veda is pretty
nearly the final expression of its own type of composition. What comes later in the way of sacred poetry

[1] Rig-Veda 8. 6. 11 ; cf. 8. 44. 12 ; 8. 76. 6.
[2] Rig-Veda 8. 95. 5.

is distinctly epigonal, or after-born.   We are face to face with the finished product of this past age.

If we consider that the theme is the worship of un-clarified polytheistic gods, but little advanced beyond the point where they originated somewhere in nature, or in a tolerably primitive consciousness, we may say, taking the fat with the lean, that the pride of these poets in their work is justified.   Of course we must not apply the chaster standards of a later time, nor can we expect perfectly even results.   Anyhow, in the poet's own eyes the Rig-Vedic hymn is a thing of blameless, finished beauty.   He has fashioned it as a skilled artisan a war chariot.   He has filed it until it is free from all blemish, "as grain is winnowed in the winnowing-basket," "as ghee is clarified for the sacri-fice."   The heart of the poets is in their work, they are unquestionably giving the best they have.   The poems are their inspirations.   In so far as they rise above their all too human interests, in so far as they are something higher than blarneying beggars, they lift themselves up through their own art rather than the intrinsic qualities of the gods upon whom they spend their efforts.

In the end the gods themselves take a hand in these valuable and delectable poetic performances.   Al-though they cannot directly furnish the metres, alliterations, beautiful words, and bold figures of speech, they can perform another service. They may furnish the devout mind, the inspiration that is behind the hymn. In fact the gods themselves perform prayers, and fashion hymns: " May the gods who perform *brahma* (that is, prayer) furnish us their thrice-covering protection from evil!"[1] "Sing ye a *brahma* given by the gods!" exhorts a poet of the house of Kanva.[2] Prayer, or devotion, is so beautiful as to be imagined dressed out in glowing colors and bright garments: " May God Agni lift up our devotion that hath glowing color!" or: " May God Agni place on high our brightly adorned devotion!"[3] Heaven and Earth, stable and orderly, guide the sacrifice, aglow with shining hymns.[4] Prayers, personified, go by the path of the divine order to the gods Indra and Agni; they are the messengers between the two worlds.[5] Hymnal beatification of prayer can scarcely reach higher than the following:

> " Prayer born of yore in heaven,
>   Eagerly chanted in the holy assembly,
>   Delightfully dressed out in bright array,
>   Ours is that father-inherited prayer of old !"
>   (Rig-Veda 3. 39. 2.)

[1] Rig-Veda 10.66. 5.
[2] *Ibid.*, I. 37. 4 ; 8. 32. 7.
[3] *Ibid.*, I. 143. 7; 144. I.
[4] *Ibid.*, 4. 56. 2.
[5] *Ibid.*, 3. 12. 7 and I. 173. 3.

The last step, namely that Prayer or Devotion itself becomes divine and assumes a tolerably distinct personality, deserves to hold our attention. The epithet "Goddess" is freely given to numerous designations of prayer and devotion. There is the "Goddess Devotion" (Dhī); the goddess "Lovely Praise" (Sushtuti); the goddess "Holy Thought" (Manīshā), and others.[1] And by an almost comical *tour de force*, such as is possible only in India, Devotion, having become divine, turns into a real personage who might in the company of the other gods call out a second layer of the same article: "Drink the soma, O ye Açvins, in the company of Agni and Indra, of Varuna and Vishnu . . . in the company of all pious Devotions."[2]

For the history of the human mind this last out-come, present in the ancient literature of this gifted people, is of unusual importance. The rather mystic idea of the divinity of Devotion and its expression, the notion that the sacred inspired thought and word can itself be god, will concern us more later on. From the point of view of religious feeling it is the last and best word of the Hindus as to the nature of the divine. There comes to mind the first verse of the Gospel of John: "In the beginning was

[1] See Rig-Veda 3. 18. 3 ; 4. 43. 1 ; 7. 34. 1 and 9 ; 8. 27. 13.
[2] *Ibid* 8. 35. 1 *ff.*

the Word, and the Word was with God, and the Word was God." Here the original Greek for " Word " is Logos. This is not quite the same as the Hindu " Devotion," or " Holy Utterance," which we shall meet again in its finished expression as Brahma. The Logos originated in the philosophy of the Stoics and the Neo-Platonists: it is intellectual rather than emotional. But the two are alike in this: they seek the creative power and the creative plan in the mind or heart of the universe rather than in its mechanical manifestations. We shall see farther on how very peculiar is the treatment which the Hindus gave to this important and original concept, led on thereto by the melancholy genius that may be supposed to preside over the hot sombre land. For the present, and in this connection, we may be satisfied to see the origin of this seemingly mystic idea exposed to our eyes with a degree of clearness that is not obscured by its mythological coloring. Like almost all other important religious ideas of the Hindus this idea, when analysed patiently with the help of their rich literature, sheds light on the seeming mysteries of other religions.

LECTURE THE FIFTH.

The Beginnings of Hindu Theosophy.

Statement of the problem—Time when theosophy originated —Metempsychosis and pessimism unknown in the earlier Vedic records—Place where the higher religion· originated—Priest philosophy at the sacrifice—The theosophic charade—Specimens of the theosophic charade—The riddle hymn of Dīrghatamas—Interrelation between the sacrifice and theosophy—On the supposed origin of theosophy with the royal caste— Criticism of this view—Transition from ritualistic polytheism to theosophy—Early scepticism—"Götterdämmerung"—Failure of God Varuna Monism, or the idea of unity—The creation hymn—Translation and analysis of the creation hymn—Attempts at monotheism—Prajāpati, the Lord of Creatures—Viçvakarman, creator of the universe, and kindred conceptions—Purusha, the world man—Brihaspati, the Lord of Devotion—Transcendental monotheistic conceptions: "Time," "Love," etc.—Defects of the earlier monotheistic and monistic attempts.

THE appreciation of the higher forms of Hinduism has gotten to be one of the foremost intellectual arts of our time, because the final results of Hindu thought count really among the most noteworthy achievements of the human mind.   In

order to understand the origin and nature of the
higher religion of the Veda it is necessary to twist
many threads into a single skein. It is a question
of when, where, by whom, and how; each phase of
this question, if considered aright, will contribute to
the clearness of the whole.

As regards the time when higher religious motives
appear, I would remind my hearers of the indefinite
and relative character of Vedic chronology. The
older Upanishads, the Vedic texts which profess
higher religion or theosophy, are written in about
the same language and style as the so-called Brāhmana texts. These latter, as you may remember,[1]
are prose works which, quite like the Hebrew Talmud, define the sacrifice with minute prescript and
illustrative legend. And the older Upanishads are
part of the Brāhmanas; the majority of the older
Upanishads, through the medium of the Āranyakas,
join their theosophic speculations right on to the
dead ritual. To some extent the bones of the ritual
skeleton rattle about in early theosophy in quite a
lively fashion. The Upanishads and theosophy are
part of the Veda; neither Hindu believer nor western critic has ever doubted that. Now the thought
of the Upanishads has its forerunners in all parts of
Vedic literature clear back to the Rig-Veda; in the

[1] See above, p. 43.

14

Atharva-Veda it even shows signs of at least temporary going to seed.[1] We cannot expect the family-books of the Rig-Veda, or the ninth, *soma* book to break out in theosophy. These books are collections of hymns addressed to the gods at a definite sacrifice : to that business they attend. It does not follow that what they do not mention does not exist at that time. We must beware of too straight-lined a view of these matters, one type following another like a row of bricks, or like different troops of the same army. I am not wise enough to say when the following stanza was pronounced : " They call (it) Indra, Mitra, Varuna, and Agni, or the heavenly bird Garutmant (the Sun). The sages call the One Being in many ways ; they call it Agni, Yama, Mātariçvan."

This verse states that the great gods of the Veda are but One Being ; therefore it at once takes a high stand in the range of possible human thought. And yet it occurs in a hymn of the Rig-Veda, namely, the famous riddle-hymn of Dīrghatamas, in the first book of that collection.[2] Another statement in the tenth book[3] is as follows : " That One breathed

---

[1] Some stanzas of the Atharvan occupy the most advanced position of the Upanishads. For instance, 10. 8. 44 : " Free from desire, true, eternal, self-begotten, full of joy, subject to none, he no longer fears death who knows the wise, ageless Ātman."

[2] Rig-Veda I. 164. 46.   [3] Rig-Veda 10. 129. 2.

without breath, by inner power; than it, truly, nothing whatever else existed besides."

Here are two statements in two Brahmanical hymns, composed in the *trishtubh* metre, the same metre in which the Vedic poets love to call upon their fustian god Indra, and yet their intention is unmistakable. They herald monism; they claim that there is but one essence, one true thing: it is but a step from such ideas to the pantheistic, absolute, without a second, Brahman-Ātman of the Upanishads and the later Vedānta philosophy.

On the other hand, there are in the earlier religion, whether it be hymn and sacrifice to the gods, or theosophic thought, no clear signs of belief in the transmigration of souls; no pessimistic view of life, and consequently no scheme of salvation, or rather release (*mukti*) from the eternal round of existences, in which birth, old age, decay, and death are the nodal points in the chain of lives. That this phase of the higher religion belongs to a later time, to a different geographical locality, and to an economic and social state different from that of the earliest Vedic time, seems exceedingly likely. So we are led to the conclusion that there was a period of monistic speculation, tentative in character, yet fairly advanced at the time of the composition of at least the later hieratic hymns of the Rig-Veda. But this higher religious thought lacked the twin factors of metempsychosis and pessimism which really determine its Hindu character. Pessimist view of transmigration, and release from transmigration are the true signs of Hinduisn in the broadest sense of that word: through these twin conceptions the Hindu idea, as we may call it, is marked off from all the rest of human thought; without these, Hindu speculations about the divine might readily pose as a kind of Volapük, or Esperanto, for all the world of religious thought from the Prophets and Plato to Spinoza and Kant. We may safely date the entrance of metempsychosis and pessimism towards the end, rather than the beginning of Vedic tradition. It seems to mark a most important division of the Veda into two periods. Other marks, such as more or less advanced priestly ritual; the presence or absence of complicated witchcraft practices; the sudden and unexpected glint of a brilliant theosophic idea; or the varying forms of Vedic literary tradition involve real distinctions of time, but they are more gradual, and are easily construed subjectively. They do not, at any rate, involve anything as vital as the presence or absence of that pessimist doctrine of transmigration which holds India captive—to its cost—even at the present day.

Next, where did the higher religion spring up

There is at this time no centre of learning, no stoa, no monastery, no university. With the beginning of the growth of the higher religion there are connected many names, but not *one* name. There is no great teacher of genius like Buddha who is of a later time. We have no reason to look to some confined space within which this business of world philosophy was carried on exclusively. Indeed, the sporadic, tentative nature of the earliest high thought, the way in which it was approached from many different sides and in many different moods, shows that it flitted about from place to place, and was the play-ball of many minds. But, I believe, we can tell pretty definitely the kind of environment from which theosophy received its first impulse, and within which it prospered up to goodly size and strength. That, curiously enough, was the great Vedic sacrifice with its mock business and endless technicalities, calculated to deaden the soul, and apparently the very thing to put the lid tight on higher religious inspiration and aspiration.

The great Vedic sacrifices, the so-called *çrauta* sacrifices, such as the *rājasūya* (coronation of a king), or the *açvamedha* (horse-sacrifice) were performances intended to strengthen the temporal power of kings. They were, of course, undertaken either by kings or at least rich Kshatriyas, rather than by the class of smaller house-holders who could not afford them, and did not have any use for them.   They had in them the elements of public, tribal or national festivals.[1] Of course they were expensive.   A large number of priests were present.   We have seen in the past that these gentlemen were not at all shy about asking fees (*dakshiṇā*) for their services.   Now we are told distinctly that the Vedic Kings, or tribal Rājas, were not only interested in the mechanical perfection and outward success of the sacrifices undertaken under their patronage, but that they were even more impressed by the speculative, mystic, and theosophic thoughts which were suggested by various phases of the sacrifice.   Both in the Brāhmanas and in the Upanishads kings appear as questioners of the great Brahmans who solve for them some knotty sacrificial problem, or even some question connected with the riddle of existence.   Whenever their questions are answered to their satisfaction, in the midst of a continuous discourse, the King again and again is excited to generosity: " I give thee a thousand (cows)," says King Janaka of Videha to the great theosopher Yājnavalkya, as the latter unfolds his marvellous scheme of salvation in the " Great Forest Upanishad."[2]   Kings were known to give away their

[1] *Cf.* Ludwig, *Der Rig-Veda*, vol. vi., p. x.
[2] Brihadāranyaka Upanishad 4. 13. 14 *ff*.

kingdoms on such occasions, and kings became themselves glorious expounders of theosophic religion.

The beginnings of theosophic thought are not in
the Upanishads but, as we have said before, in the
polytheistic and ritualistic religion that preceded the
Upanishad. Especially in connection with the great
sacrifices of the kind just mentioned the Brahmans,
in the long run, found it to their advantage to
impress the " generous givers," the patrons of the sacrifice, not only with their mastery of sacrificial technique, but also with their theological profundity. To
some extent learned theological discussions in prose,
of a highly scholastic (Talmudic) nature, fulfil this purpose. This we may call the philosophy of the sacrifice, such as is displayed, for instance, in the exposition of the *agnihotra* sacrifice in Çatapatha Brāhmana
11. 6. 2. But furthermore, they employ a very interesting form of poetic riddle or charade to enliven
the mechanical and technical progress of the sacrifice
by impressive intellectual pyrotechnics. I question
whether such a type of religious literature is known
in any other religion, or whether the riddle has ever
elsewhere been drafted into the service of religion
as one of the stages of its advancement. In other
words, religious charades are a part of Hindu religious literature.[1]

[1] See Haug, *Vedische Räthselfragen und Räthselsprüche, Transac-*

The Vedic word for higher speculative discussion as a whole, and especially for the religious, mostly poetic, riddle is *brahmodya* or *brahmavadya*, that is, "analysis or speculation about the *brahma*, or religion." It is very generally carried on by two priests, one of whom asks questions, the other answers them. It is a kind of theological "quiz," prearranged by the two parties: questioner and responder know their parts to perfection.

At the horse-sacrifice two priests ask and answer:

"Who, verily, moveth quite alone; who, verily, is born again and again; what, forsooth, is the remedy for cold; and what is the great (greatest) pile"?

The answer is:

"The sun moveth quite alone; the moon is born again and again; Agni (fire) is the remedy for cold; the earth is the great (greatest) pile." [1]

The priest called Hotar asks the priest called Adhvaryu:

"What, forsooth, is the sun-like light; what sea is there like unto the ocean; what, verily, is higher than the earth; what is the thing whose measure is not known"?

The answer is:

"Brahma is the sun-like light; heaven is the sea like

---

tions of the Munich Academy, 1875, p. 7 *ff.* of the reprint; Ludwig, *Der Rig-Veda*, vol. iii., p. 390 *ff.*; the author, *Journal of the American Oriental Society*, vol. xv., p. 172.

[1] Vājasaneyi Samhitā 23. 9 and 10.

unto the ocean ; (the god) Indra is higher than the earth ; the measure of the cow is (quite) unknown. '[1]

Again the following questions and answers :

" I ask thee for the highest summit of the earth ; I ask thee for the navel of the universe ; I ask thee for the seed of the lusty steed ; I ask thee for the highest heaven of speech."

" This altar is the highest summit of the earth ; this sacrifice is the navel of the universe ; this *soma* (the intoxicating sacrificial drink) is the seed of the lusty steed (God Indra ?) ; this Brahman priest is the highest heaven (that is to say, the highest exponent) of speech. "[2]

It is interesting to note that these riddles show us again the Hindu mind preoccupied with the nature phenomena of the world, at a time when the old nature gods have become completely crystallised. Again, as regards the status of these riddles, the Kena Upanishad opens with a very similar pair of riddle-stanzas, showing that the state of mind at the bottom of nature-worship, *brahmodya*, and Upanishad marks advancing mental interests, but yet advance along the same line.

The Rig-Veda (1. 164) contains a hymn which is nothing but a collection of fifty-two verses of poetry, all of them, except one, riddles whose answers are not given. There can be little doubt that the occa-

[1] The same text, 23. 47 and 48.
[2] *Ibid.*, 23. 61 and 62.

sion upon which these riddles were let off was the same as with those just cited, namely, the sacrifice. The subjects of these riddles are cosmic, that is, pertaining to the nature phenomena of the universe; mythological. that is, referring to the accepted legends about the gods; psychological, that is, pertaining to the human organs and sensations; or, finally, crude and tentative philosophy or theosophy. Heaven and earth, sun and moon, air, clouds and rain; the course of the sun, the year, the seasons, months, days and nights; the human voice, self-consciousness, life and death; the origin of the first creature and the originator of the universe—such are the abrupt and bold themes. Here figures also (stanza 46) that seemingly precocious statement which contains the suggestion, symptomatic for all future Hindu thought, namely, that above and behind the great multitude of gods there is one supreme personality; behind the gods there is that " Only Being " of whom the gods are but various names—πολλῶν ὀνομάτων μορφὴ μία:

" They call it Indra, Mitra, Varuna, and Agni, or the heavenly bird Garutmant (the sun). The sages call the One Being in many ways ; they call it Agni, Yama, Mātariçvan."

How closely attached to the sacrifice theosophic speculations remained as they grew in clearness and importance, we cannot say ; all that we can say is, that in time the two intrinsically uncongenial themes parted company. Nor can we assert that theosophic thought would not have sprung up in the Hindu mind, endowed as we see it to be, independently from the sacrifice and its perverted scholastic scintillations. Given the mind, the thought will come. But it is easy to see that the beginnings of higher religion started around the sacrifice, by calling out the higher aspirations of the patrons of the sacrifice. Wisdom-searching Rājas, weary of the world, Janaka and Ajātaçatru at an earlier time, Buddha and Bimbisāra at a later time, have as much to do with the development of Hindu religion as the thirst for newer and larger truth on the part of the Brahmans themselves. The Rājas were the Mæcenases of the "poor clerics." We imagine very easily that some of them got a surfeit of the world, and were attracted to the things beyond. The beginnings of theosophy grew up around the sacrifice which was under their patronage. The Brahmans grew up to their patrons' —and, we may add, to their own—higher needs. They began to offer these patrons something more than ritual technicalities. In the long run they must hold their position and reputation by something better than by handling with ludicrous correctness fire-wood and sacrificial ladle ; *soma* drink and oblations of melted butter. And in the long run their minds, which somehow, the hocus-pocus of the sacrifice had neither deadened nor satisfied, rose to those higher and permanent requirements which led to practical abandonment of the sacrifice and lasting devotion to philosophic religion.

The question, next, as to who carried on the higher religion has been answered incidentally in what has just been said. If what is stated there is stated correctly, we shall not go astray if we assume that the Brahmans were the mainspring in the advance of higher thought, just as they were the main factors in the worship of the gods and in ceremonial practices. But this same question requires to be stated more precisely for the following reason. A number of distinguished scholars have recently advanced the theory that Hindu theosophy is not, as has been tacitly assumed, in the main the product of Brahmanical intellect, but that it was due to the spiritual insight of the Royal or Warrior Caste.[1]

Professor Garbe of the University of Tübingen, an eminent student of Hindu philosophy and at the same time a scholar well versed in the early literature of the Vedas, is the most ardent advo-

[1] See Deussen, *Allgemeine Geschichte der Philosophie*, vol. i., part 2, pp. 354 *ff.*; Garbe, *Beiträge zur Indischen Kulturgeschichte*, pp. 3 *ff* ; Winternitz, *Geschichte der Indischen Litteratur*, pp. 196 *ff*.

cate of this view. Garbe is not at all an admirer
of Brahman civilisation; on more than one occasion has he poured out the vials of his just
wrath against the intolerable pretensions and cruel-
ties which the Brahmans have practised during the
period of their ascendancy in India through several
milleniums. But not content with that, he believes
that the Brahmans were not only bold bad men, but
also that they were too stupid to have worked their
way from the sandy wastes of ritualism to the green
summits where grows the higher thought of India.
For centuries the Brahmans were engaged in ex-
cogitating sacrifice after sacrifice, and hair-splitting
definitions and explanations of senseless ritualistic
hocus-pocus. "All at once," says Professor Garbe,
"lofty thought appears upon the scene. To be
sure, even then the traditional god-lore, sacrificial
lore, and folk-lore are not rejected, but the spirit is
no longer satisfied with the cheap mysteries that
surround the sacrificial altar. A passionate desire
to solve the riddle of the universe and its relation to
the own self holds the mind captive; nothing less
will satisfy henceforth."

Parts of this observation of Professor Garbe are
correct, nay even familiar. But not every part, it
seems to me. Having in mind Yājnavalkya and
Uddālaka Āruni of the Upanishads, or Çankara and

Kumārila of the Vedānta Philosophy, one may fairly doubt the unredeemed stupidity of the Brahmans at any period of India's history. I would, for my part, question more particularly the expression "all at once" in the above statement.

Mental revolutions rarely come all at once, least of all in India. The evidence of India's remarkably continuous records shows that every important Hindu thought has its beginning, middle, and final development. As regards theosophy, its beginnings are found in the Vedic hymns; its middle in the Upanishads; and its final development in the "Systems" of Philosophy, like the Vedānta and Sānkhya of later times. I am afraid that Professor Garbe has somehow gotten into the state of mind that there is only one kind of good Brahman, namely, a dead Brahman, to paraphrase a saying about that other Indian, the American Indian. Selfishness, foolishness, bigotry, and cruelty galore—the marks of these *some* Brahmans have left in their compositions, foolishly as behooves knaves. But there were, and there are, Brahmans and Brahmans. The older Upanishads, written in approximately the same language and style as the so-called prose Brāhmana (Talmudic) texts, figuring largely as parts of these compositions, were composed by Brahmans who had risen to the conviction that not "the way of works" lies the salvation that is knowledge. Countless Brahman names crowd these texts: Naciketas and Çvetaketu, Gārgya and Yājnavalkya, and many others. Even the wives or daughters of great Brahmans, Gārgī and Maitreyī, take part in spiritual tourneys, and occasionally, as in the case of Gārgī in the Great Forest-Upanishad (3. 6 and 8), rise to a subtler appreciation than the Brahman men of the mystery of the world and the riddle of existence.

The scholars mentioned have been attracted to their position by the interesting fact that the Upanishads narrate several times that the ultimate philosophy was in the keeping of men of royal caste, and that these warriors imparted their knowledge to Brahmans. This is put in such a way that the Brahman, after having aired his own stock of theosophy "lays down" before the king's superior insight. The king is then represented as graciously bestowing his saving knowledge upon the Brahman. Once or twice, however, the king turns braggart, and mars his generosity by claiming that the warrior caste are the real thing, and that they alone in all the world are able to illumine these profound and obscure matters. Thus the extreme example of this kind is narrated in two Upanishads.[1] The Brahman Çvetaketu Āruni, ignorant of the doctrine of transmigration, is com-

[1] Brihad Āranyaka Upanishad 6. 2 ; Chāndogya Upanishad 5. 3.

pelled to look for instruction to King Pravāhana
Jaivali, who receives him graciously and condescends
to become his teacher.   In the course of his preach-
ment the King says to the Brahman :

" Because, as thou hast told me, this doctrine ere this
and up to thy time has not been in vogue among the
Brahmans, therefore in all the world sovereignty has remained in the hands of the warrior caste.   As surely as
we desire that thou and all thy ancestors shall remain
well-disposed towards us, so surely has to this day
no Brahman ever possessed this knowledge."

I doubt whether this statement, and others of
a similar nature, justify us in regarding the warrior
caste as the spiritual saviors of India.   As regards
King Pravāhana Jaivali's statement, it is specious on
the face of it.   For what have royalty and transmigration to do with one another?   In its essence the
doctrine of transmigration has no more regard for
royalty than for the lowest caste, because its purpose
is release from any form of individual existence (see
the sixth lecture).   Then again, the very texts that
narrate these exploits of the Kshatriyas are unquestionably Brahmanic.   Would the arrogance and
selfishness of the Brahmans have allowed them to
preserve and propagate facts calculated to injure
permanently their own standing?   Surely not.

The situation is somewhat as follows : there never

was a time in India when the Aryas, that is,
the three upper of the four ancient castes, were
excluded from Brahmanical piety.¹ Now, as theosophy, by its very terms, shuts down on the ritual,
the special profession of the Brahmans, there is
nothing at all in it to exclude occasional intelligent
and aspiring men from the other noble (Arya) castes.
This is true even at the present day : Svāmī Vive-
kānanda was no Brahman, but a member of the
Kayastha or clerk caste.   The Chāndogya Upanishad (4. 4) narrates how Satyakāma, the son of
the gadabout servant-maid Jabālā, was admitted to
Brahmanic disciplehood by Hāridrumata, for the
very reason that he did not try to cover up his low
birth.   Satyakāma, in the end, obtains the highest
knowledge.   When it comes to higher religion the
bars are consciously let down at all times.   In the
Mokshadharma of the Mahābhārata² the Vaiçya
(Vanik) caste man Tulādhāra, "seller of juices, scents,
leaves, barks, fruits, and roots," teaches righteousness to the Brahman Jājali.   In the same text³ the
Rishi Parāçara declares that Brahmans learned in the
Veda regard a virtuous Çūdra, or low caste man, as
the equal of Brahmans.

---

¹ Compare Pandit Shyāmaji Krishnavarma, *Transactions of the
Fifth International Congress of Orientalists*, vol. ii., p. 218 *ff.*
² 12. 261 *ff.*   ³ 12. 290 *ff.*
15

Here, I think, is where the good Brahman, of whom Professor Garbe will not hear, comes in. The Brahman authors of the Upanishads, just as high-minded Brahmans of all ages, were honest and liberal enough to permit all fit men to participate in higher religious activity, in wisdom and in piety. Nay, they express particular admiration in such participation, because, after all, there was to them something unexpected in all this. They were carried away by it to a certain ecstasy, the kind of ecstasy that goes with a paradox, as when the son of a peasant in Europe works his way to a professorship in a university. As regards the Rājas, or other nobles, we must not forget, too, that they were after all the source from which all blessings flowed. Even in theosophic occupation the Brahman remains, as I have said before, the poor cleric with the Rāja as his Mæcenas. I think that any one who reads these statements of royal proficiency in the highest wisdom attentively will acknowledge that they are dashed in the Upanishads, as they are in the Ritual, with a goodly measure of *captatio benevolentiæ*. In other words, the genuine admiration of high-minded nobles is not necessarily divorced from the subconsciousness that it is well to admire in high places. Even really good Brahmans might do that.

If King Janaka of Videha punctuates the Brahman

Yājnavalkya's brilliant exposition of theosophy by repeated gifts of a thousand cows—we may wonder who counted them, and what Yājnavalkya did with them—King Ajātaçatru of Benares, real intellectual as he is, will not allow admiring Brahmans to starve.

I think that a saying of the modern sage and pious ascetic, the Paramahansa Rāmakrishna,[1] throws essentially the right light upon the exceptional character of the theosophic exploits of kings : " Men always quote the example of the King Janaka, as that of a man who lived in the world and yet attained perfection. But throughout the whole history of mankind there is only this solitary example. His case was not the rule but the exception." We may tone down this statement, and apply it to the present question as follows : Not all Brahmans were intellectually or morally sound, but some Brahmans were at all times, as they were in the days of Çankara and Kumārila, the intellectual leaders of India ; brilliant helpers from the other castes, more especially the Royal caste,[2] lent occasional aid, and this aid justly compelled acknowledgment and admiration.

I am now come at last to the " how " of Hindu higher thought, that is, my task is now to show how the main or essential thoughts of Hindu theosophy

[1] See Max Müller, *Rāmakrishna, His Life and Sayings*, p. 127.
[2] See above. p. 219.

arose. In the transition from the nature gods, the
legends, the ritual, and the folk-lore practices, to the
settled theosophy of later times, many conceptions
flit like phantoms across the vision of these specu-
lators or seers, sometimes not to be heard of a second
time. The air is charged with experimental, electric
thought. No religious or philosophic literature of
ancient times has buried so many " lost children " as
the Hindu in the storm and stress period that ends
with the Upanishads. No people of thinkers have
started to rear so many edifices of thought to be
abandoned without regret or scruple when found
wanting in the end. They have left behind them
many a ruin which they might well enough have
finished, and within which the religious thinkers of
many another nation, less exacting, would have
cheerfully settled upon as permanent and congenial
habitations. Philip Sidney's saying: " Reason cannot show itself more reasonable than to leave off
reasoning on things above reason," does not hold
with the Hindus. They would certainly have stig-
matised such sweet reasonableness as the philosophy
of sloth, if they had ever heard of it. On the
contrary, the old questions of whence, why, and
whither fascinate and enthrall their thoughts from
the time of the Vedic Rishis to the present day.
Remarkable as this may sound, we have really no

record of any period of Hindu thought of which we can say definitely that it was wanting in the highest and most strenuous thought, from the time of the riddle-hymn of Dirghatamas and the creation-hymn,[1] to the modern Vedāntins and Paramahansas of the type of Rāmakrishna and Vivekānanda.

To begin with, negatively speaking, there are at a very early time traces of scepticism. The old myth-ological gods in strong flesh tints are just the least bit disconcerting. There are those who begin to say of the gods : " They are not," and, doubtless, there is a growing number of those who begin to weaken in that faith (*çraddha*) which means monotonously sacrifice, and gifts to the Brahmans. The way in which the Veda insists upon this faith shows that it could not always be taken for granted. Especially the god Indra who is a good deal of a Bombastes Furioso must have presented himself to the eye of the more enlightened as a brummagem god, tricky, braggart, drunken, and immoral. Indra, like Zeus, will have his fling. There is a story about himself and a lady by the name of Ahalyā in which he assumes the outer form of that lady's august priestly husband for his own purposes, and this as well as other treacherous acts are a fruitful source of moral ising in the later Veda. Even in the Rig-Veda, if

[1] Rig-Veda 1. 164 and 10. 129.

we read between the lines, there are those who mock Indra, and those who apologise for him :

"Bring lovely praise to Indra, vying one with the other, truthful praise, if he himself be true. Even though one or another says : 'Indra is not, who ever saw him, who is he that we should praise him?'"

(Rig-Veda 8. 100 3.)

Or again :

"The terrible one of whom they ask, 'where is he?'
Nay verily they say of him, 'he is not at all'.
He makes shrink the goods of his enemy like a gambler
    the stakes of his opponent :
Put your faith in him—He, O folks, is Indra."

(Rig-Veda 2. 12 5.)

Hence they that have no faith are called *açraddha,* "infidel," or *anindra,* "repudiators of Indra."[1]

Every onward movement of Hindu thought takes place at the expense of the old gods of nature ; the divine attribute becomes more important than the mythological person. The individual natural history of the gods becomes a thing of minor interest. In this sense polytheism is decadent even in the hymns of the Rig-Veda themselves. It shows signs of going to seed for philosophy. The gods in turn perform about the same feats of creating and upholding the world : the interest of the poets in the acts has evidently increased at the expense of the

[1] Rig-Veda 7. 6. 3 and 5. 2. 3. ; 10. 48. 7.

agents. The gods, too, we must not forget, have taken, very mechanically, fixed positions in the ritual devoted to their service. One thing is certain, in the host of figures that crowd the canvass in the transition period from mythology to theosophy the nature gods play no real rôle. They are, if not exactly abandoned, at least relegated to a subordinate position and treated with comparative coldness. Every embodiment of the divine idea is now abstract or symbolic. The higher forms of early Hindu religion operate decidedly from the ontological side, from the severely intellectual side. Faith and piety, sentiment and emotion, right and wrong, invariably take the second place, as long as there is to settle the question of the universe, the great cosmos; man, the little cosmos; time; space; causality. Therefore, perhaps, the plastic possibilities of the early gods through poetry, legend, and the art of reproduction remain in India a coarse-grained exercise of second rate power: one needs but to call up for comparison the part that Greek mythology plays in Greek literature and art.

It is interesting to test this on the person of one great nature god of the early time. We have seen that in a very early prehistoric time, the common period of the Hindus and Iranians, there existed a high view of the gods as moral forces, as the omni-

scient guardians of the moral law and order of the
universe. Avestan Ahura Mazda and Vedic Varuna
are the guardians-in-chief of the *rta*, the cosmic and
moral order of the universe and man.[1] Vedic Varuna
in his ethical strength has a Hebraic flavor. By the
side of even the loftiest figure and the loftiest traits
of the Hellenic or Teutonic Pantheon Varuna stands
like a Jewish prophet by the side of a priest of
Dagon. And yet what permanent moral strength
have the Hindus derived from Varuna, and what becomes of Varuna himself in the course of his development? A second rate Neptune, " Lord of the
Waters," a mere stage figure. In the straight-lined
advance, looking neither to the right nor to the left,
to the recognition of the one Brahma, the universal
spirit, as the one Reality, and the consequent illu-
soriness of the entire phenomenal world, there is
really no more room for righteous and stern Varuna
than for an idol of clay, unless you can make out
that Varuna is but a particular manifestation of the
One Brahma, and then he is no more important than
. any other manifestation.

The absence of a strong chronological scaffolding
is felt not only for the events of Hindu history, but
also for the events of Hindu thought. It is the custom to speak rather glibly of " late " and " early " in

[1] See above, p. 126.

these thought movements. As a matter of fact we are at the beginning of higher Hindu thought confronted with its most important and most permanent idea. Some poets of the Vedic time, writing, not badly, in Vedic metre, see more or less clearly that the idea of God, in so far as it can be conceived at all, presupposes the idea of absolute unity. It is a thought both independent and of leonine boldness. Independent, because there is no suspicion of foreign thinkers, or foreign literature. Bold, because it will soon lead to the conclusion that there is but one real thing, one "That," one *ding an sich*, which exists both in the universe and in man, and that all else is illusion. Whatever else we may say of this conception, a bolder conception has not emanated from the brain of man; a bolder conception cannot, perhaps, come from the brain of man. We have become acquainted with one expression of this unity in the hymn of Dīrghatamas[1]: "They call it Indra, Mitra, Varuna, and Agni, or the heavenly bird Garutmant (the sun). The sages call the one being in many ways; they call it Agni, Yama, Mātariçvan." Professor Deussen, in his History of Philosophy,[2] remarks that no more epoch-marking word has been uttered in India until we come to the famous *tat tvam asi,*

[1] Rig-Veda 1.164.46.
[2] *Allgemeine Geschichte der Philosophie*, vol. i., part i, p. 106.

" thou art the That," of the Chāndogya Upanishad.
Lest some one should suspect this to be a mere
blundering thought for the nonce, a kind of freak or
sport of mental rumination, the same Dīrghatamas
hymn contains the idea several times more; for
instance in stanza 6:

" In ignorance do I ask here them that haply know,
    Who did support the six regions of the world ?
    What was, forsooth, this one unborn thing " ?

The tenth book of the Rig-Veda contains the
famous creation hymn (10.129). This remarkable
production has always interested Sanskritists profoundly; it has also passed over into the general
literature of religion and philosophy. That great and
sober critic, the late Professor William D. Whitney,
remarked anent it in 1882, that the unlimited praises
which had been bestowed upon it, as philosophy and
as poetry, were well-nigh nauseating.[1] And yet,
twelve years later, in 1894, Deussen, who, I am sure,
is not trying to contradict Whitney, breaks out into
new praise, more ecstatic than ever: " In its noble
simplicity, in the loftiness of its philosophic vision
it is possibly the most admirable bit of philosophy of
olden times." And again, " No translation can ever
do justice to the beauty of the original."[2]   I think

[1] *Proceedings of the American Oriental Society*, vol. xi., p. cxi.
[2] *History of Philosophy*, vol. i., part i, pp. 119 and 126.

we may grant that the composition shows a good deal of rawness, unevenness, and inconsistency. Yet it is perhaps easier to undervalue such a performance than to exaggerate its importance. It occurs in one of the earliest literatures of the world ; it brushes aside all mythology, and it certainly exhibits philosophic depth and caution when it designates the fundamental cause of the universe not by a name, but as " that " (*tad*), or " the one thing " (*ekam*). But let my hearers judge for themselves :

FIRST STANZA.

" *Nor being was there nor non-being ; there was no atmosphere and no sky beyond. What covered all, and where, by what protected ? Was there a fathomless abyss of the waters ?* "

The poet describes as deftly as possible a primordial chaos. There was not non-being, for that is unconceivable [1] ; there was not being in the ordinary experience of the senses. What was there? The poet in the next stanza carries on his negation and then abruptly presses forward to a positive conclusion :

SECOND STANZA.

" *Neither death was there nor immortality ; there*

[1] *Cf.* Chāndogya Upanishad 6. 2. 2.

was not the sheen of night nor light of day. That One breathed, without breath, by inner power ; than it truly nothing whatever else existed besides."

The poet is careful in his thought of what positively was. It is " That One " (*tad ekam*) ; it exists and breathes, but it breathes in a higher sense, without breath (literally " wind ") which is physical and material. It is difficult to imagine a more cautious, or even a more successful attempt to conceive and express a first cause or principle without personality. Yet we must not fail to observe that even so subtle a conception as the neuter " That One " is furnished with the anthropomorphic attribute of breath, because after all, in the long run, it must be decked out in some sort of flesh and blood. The third stanza takes up anew the description of chaos, and follows it up with a second description of the primal force :

THIRD STANZA.

" *Darkness there was, hidden by darkness at the beginning ; an unillumined ocean was this all. The living force which was enveloped in a shell, that one by the might of devotional fervor was born."*

Unquestionably we have here the idea, frequently expressed in the Brāhmana tales of the creator Prajāpati.[1] According to this the primal being be-

[1] See below, p. 240.

gins to create through the force of devotion (*tapas*).
Here an even more primary condition is assumed :
the fundamental force is itself put forth by, or is
born from, devotion. This devotional fervor marks
either another start at a primeval cause, or, paradox-
ical as this may seem, is the devotional fervor of the
yet uncreated sages. Anyhow these sages appear
upon the scene as *dei ex machina* in the next stanza,
and then, after this gap has been spanned, the work
of creation can really proceed.

FOURTH STANZA.

"*Desire arose in the beginning in That ; it was the
first seed of mind. The sages by devotion found the
root of being in non-being, seeking it in (their) heart.*"

Desire, Kāma, the equivalent of Greek Ἔρως
" Love," means here the desire to live ; it is the first
possible seed or fruit of the mind, for there is no
conceivable action of the mind which is not preceded
by life. The second hemistich introduces an even
more primordial creative rôle on the part of the
sages, whose devotion is the real promotive force in
the act of creation. The poet does not tell whence
come the sages at this stage of the drama. The
production of this creation, which is here defined as
" being " coming out of " non-being," contradicts,
the first stanza where " non-being " is denied : " How

can 'being come out of 'non-being?'" asks the Chāndogya Upanishad (6. 2. 2). Moreover it ignores the previously postulated "That Only" which by its terms eliminates "non-being." The poet here unquestionably entangles himself in sham-profundity ; he had better left out all reference to "non-being"; it is a term handled by the Hindus with a degree of deftness which is in the inverse ratio to their fondness for it.

The hymn continues with a mystical fifth stanza which is obscure, and in any case unimportant. Then it takes a wholly new turn into the direction of philosophic scepticism. This is quite unexpected in the wake of "That Only," in whose mind creative desire had sprung forth : it ought to, aided by its own or the sages' creative fervor, go on to create the world, if it does anything at all :

SIXTH STANZA.

" *Who truly knoweth ? Who can here proclaim it ?*
Whence hither born, whence cometh this creation ?
On this side are the gods from its creating,
Who knoweth then from whence it came to being ? "

SEVENTH STANZA.

"*This creation—from whence it came to being,*
Whether it made itself, or whether not—
He who is its overseer in highest heaven,
He surely knoweth—or perchance he knoweth not."

The avowed purpose of all philosophy is to account for the presence of the world and its contents, as something which is not self-evident, and needs to be explained beyond the point of mere individual experience, or analysis through empirical knowledge. The creation hymn performs this act not without some unsteadiness and with petulance due to scepticism. In putting forth a fundamental principle without personality it does not fall far behind the best thought of later times inside or outside of India. It fails where all philosophy fails, in bridging over to this particular idealistic or phenomenal world, even after the fundamental principle has been abstracted, no matter in how rarefied and non-committal a form. We may expect, therefore, other starts towards the same end. The Veda, as I have hinted before, contains an astonishing number of attempts to establish a supreme monotheistic being who is far easier to handle than the monistic "That Only"; a monotheistic god who, when once conceived, conveniently assumes all responsibility. We have seen more than once how supreme divine action makes a show of gradually detaching itself from the persons of the various gods who figure in the earlier myth and cult, and how this action impresses itself upon the mind as really more important than the particular divine agent who was at any given time supposed

to perform it. Creation of the world ; production of
the sun ; spreading out of the sky and the earth ;
and lordship over all that moves or stands—these
are some of the grander acts in world life. Even in
the Rig-Veda these acts are bunched and thrown
into the lap of a divinity by the name of Prajāpati
" Lord of Creatures." Various earlier divinities of
a more or less abstract and specialistic character,
especially Savitar, the inspiring, enlivening principle
of the sun, and Tvashtar, a kind of divine carpenter
or artificer of less important objects, are blended in
this product ; it goes as far to realise personal monotheism as was ever possible in India. One hymn[1]
pictures Prajāpati in very glowing colors ; he is
a true creator, ruler, and preserver, and yet, it is
very interesting to observe, that the description of
him does not, after all, differ very materially from that
of the polytheistic god Indra in the hymn, Rig-Veda
2. 12, as may be seen from a comparison of the two.[2]
Some of the stanzas of the Prajāpati hymn are as
follows :

Rig-Veda 10. 121.

1. " A golden germ arose in the beginning,
    Born he was the one lord of things existing,
    The earth and yonder sky he did establish—
    What god shall we revere with our oblation ?

[1] Rig-Veda 10. 121.
[2] See Deussen, *Geschichte der Philosophie*, vol. i., part i, p. 128 *ff*.

2. "Who gives life's breath and is of strength the giver,
   At whose behest all gods do act obedient,
   Whose shadow is immortality and likewise death—
   What god shall we revere with our oblation?

3. "The king, who as it breathes and as it shuts its eyes,
   The world of life alone doth rule with might,
   Two-footed creatures and four-footed both controls—
   What god shall we revere with our oblation?

4. "Through whose great might arose these snow-capped
      mountains,
   Whose are, they say, the sea and heavenly river,
   Whose arms are these directions of the space—
   What god shall we revere with our oblation?"

Not until we come to the tenth stanza does this omnipotent god who so far has not betrayed his name, unless we so regard the epithet "Golden Germ" in the first stanza, reveal himself as Prajāpati:

10. "'Prajāpati, thou art the one—and there's no other—
    Who dost encompass all these born entities!
    Whate'er we wish while offering thee oblations,
    May that be ours! May we be lords of riches!"

It is easy to feel both the inferiority and the greater convenience of this Creator God who lords it over everything, without exactly having established any particular mental or moral claim to his prerogatives. As compared with the sheer philosophic "That Only," the one thing without humanly

16

definable quality, Prajāpati cuts a sorry figure, and
marks a backward movement.   There are, as we
have said, many other monotheistic conceptions,
symbolic, ritualistic, and philosophic, which make a
short spurt and fall by the way. The supreme being
is conceived as Viçvakarman, " fabricator of the
universe "; as Parameshthin, " he who occupies the
highest summit "; as Svayambhū, " the self-exist-
ing being "; as Skambha, " Support "; as Dhātar,
"Maker "; as Vidhātar, " Arranger "; and others.
These are mere symbolism.

In another way a move in the direction of monotheistic pantheism is made through the personification of all nature as a giant " man," called Purusha.
His head is heaven, his eye is the sun, his breath is
the wind, and so on. Purusha reminds us of the
cosmic giant, Ymir in the Edda. The notion that
man is a microcosm, or small world, and that, conversely, the world is a huge man (macranthropos) is
widely diffused. Here are some stanzas of Rig-
Veda 10. 90 :

    1. " The Purusha with thousand heads,
       With thousand eyes and thousand feet,
       Surrounds the earth on every side,
       And goes ten digits yet beyond.

    2. " Purusha, aye, is all this world,
       The world that was and that will be.

He even rules th' immortal world
Which must sustain itself by food.

3. "Thus great is this his majesty—
    Yet even beyond in strength he goes.
    A quarter of him all beings are.
    Three quarters are immortal beyond."

The most significant of all monotheistic personifications is derived from the sphere of worship and ritual, namely the God Brihaspati or Brahmanaspati, "Lord of Prayer or Devotion." He presents himself at first as a mere personification of the acts of the poets and priests. We remember a preceding statement that the Vedic poets' consciousness is invaded by and impressed with the dignity and charm of their own poetic devotions. They go so far as to lift this very devoutness to the level of divinity. In Brihaspati we have a personification of prayer and religious performance both in one. A beautiful stanza of the Rig-Veda [2] has it: "When, O Brihaspati, men first sent forth the earliest utterance of speech, giving names to things, then was disclosed a jewel treasured within them, most excellent and pure." In another famous hymn of the Rig-Veda [3] Vāc, "Holy Speech," is represented as the companion and upholder of the gods, and as the foundation of

[1] See above, p. 206.   [2] 10. 71.1   [3] 10. 125

all religious activity and its attendant boons. From a later time we have the significant metaphoric statement that " Holy Song " (Dhenā) is the wife of Brihaspati just as " Weapon " (Senā) is the wife of Indra.[1]

Brihaspati at first is placed as an ally by the side of the more regal gods, like Indra, Agni, and Soma, in their fights against demons and stingy unbelievers. The Vedic gods derive strength from prayer and sacrifice, just as do Hindu men—this is a familiar conception from the beginning. The thought which underlies Brihaspati has in store for itself a greater future and a more permanent result in the still more abstract Brahma, which is religious devotion in the absolute. Of this in the last lecture. For the present Brihaspati rises from his modest position as aider and abettor of the war-gods to become father of the gods, upholder of the ends of the earth. Sun and moon's alternate rise is his work. Like a blacksmith Brihaspati soldered together this world. That happened before the races of the gods came into being ; perhaps at the time when " being " was born of " non-being."

More transcendental are the exploitations in the direction of monotheism of such conceptions

[1] See the author, *Journal of the German Oriental Society*, vol. xlviii., p. 599.

as Kāla, " Time," "Father Time"; of Kāma, "Love,"
"Eros"; of Prāna " Breath of Life "; and others even
more faint and tentative. The conception of Eros
we have met above as the first movement in The
One after it had come into life; its deification is never
very pronounced. Prāna, or " Breath of Life," is an
almost universal cosmic principle; it will occupy our
attention in connection with the final shaping of
Hindu theosophy. The most transcendental of these
personifications is that of " Time"—namely: Prajāpati, " the lord of creatures," at first an abstraction,
is readily associated with the generative power of
nature. Now this generative power is revealed particularly in the cycle of the year. By easy association Prajāpati is next boldly identified with year:
" Prajāpati reflected, ' This verily, 1 have created as
my counterpart, namely, the year.' Therefore they
say, ' Prajāpati is the year,' for as counterpart of
himself he did create the year." Thus the prose
Brāhmana texts naively, yet closely, reason. And
out of some such reasoning " Time " itself emerges
as a monotheistic conception, in whose praise the
Atharva-Veda sings two hymns [1]:

"Time runs, a steed with seven reins, thousand-eyed,
ageless, rich in seed. The seers thinking holy thoughts,
mount him ; all the beings are his wheels.

[1] 19. 53 and 54.

"Time begot yonder heaven, Time also these earths.
That which was and that which shall be, urged forth by
Time, spreads out."

(Atharva-Veda 19. 53. 1 and 5.)

After a survey of these manifold, all of them more
or less shaky attempts to account for the universe
and man, one impression, which I have spoken of before, grows mightily. I mean the presence of intellectual subtlety, the absence of sentiment. Anything
like a practical bearing of all these earlier monotheistic and monistic creations upon the Hindu mind
and heart seem as yet almost altogether wanting.
In a sense they are not religious, but crudely philosophical. That is, if we define religion as the intimate, mutual, personal relation between man and the
higher powers that surround him. In so far as they
are religious in this sense these monotheistic and
monistic creations do not advance perceptibly beyond the stage of the polytheistic nature gods, the
ritual, and the sorcery of earlier times. The extravagant power of Prajāpati is still nothing more than a
cause for cajolery:

"Prajāpati thou art the one—and there's no other—
Who dost encompass all these born entities!
Whate'er we wish, while offering thee oblations,
May that be ours !   May we be lords of riches ! "

(Rig-Veda 10. 121.10.)

All this is far from being the final form of the

higher religion. When Hindu theosophy has reached
its full growth and has stretched its limbs we find
that all its various intellectual movements still keep
on differing among themselves considerably, to the
end, as they did at the beginning. But they are
absolutely agreed on one point, namely, their final
purpose. Their final purpose is salvation ; release
from the endless chain of existences in which death
marks the passage from link to link. This salvation
can be effected in only one way, namely, profound
and genuinely religious appreciation of the identity
of one's own self with the One True Being. This
rests upon the twin doctrine of Transmigration and
Monism without which India would not be India.
The earlier forms of monotheistic and monistic
speculation show no sign of a belief in transmigration. I thought it advisable to let this belief mark
the division between the tentative, purely speculative philosophy of the earlier time, and the thought
of the Upanishads, which is in its essence truly religious. The Upanishads, with all their curvy movements and through all their fluttering thought, never
lose sight of that great purpose of salvation. How
came the belief in transmigration in India; how it
led to a pessimistic view of life ; how Brahma, the
One, the Universal, the True, finally shaped himself
from out of the mass of conflicting and yet converg-

ing thoughts about the Divine which we have sketched to-day ; and how release from the chain of existences through union with Brahma may be obtained—that will be the theme of our concluding lecture on the religion of the Veda.

LECTURE THE SIXTH.

The Final Philosophy of the Veda.

Death and future life in paradise—Early notions of Hell—
The idea of retribution—Limit of reward for good deeds
—The notion of "death-anew," or "re-death"—How
comes the belief in transmigration—Hindu doctrine
of transmigration—The method of transmigration—
The doctrine of *karma*, or spiritual evolution—How
transmigration and *karma* appear to Western minds
—The pessimist theory of life—Cause of Hindu pessimism—Pessimism and the perfect principle (Brahma)
—Dualistic pessimism—Salvation through realisation
of one's own Brahmahood—The conception of the
ātman, "breath," as life principle—Atman, the soul
of the Universe—Brahma, the spiritual essence of the
Universe—Fusion of Ātman and Brahma—Māyā, or
the world an illusion—The unknowableness of Brahma
--Emerson's poem on the Brahma—The fulness of
Brahma: a story of Yājnavalkya and his wife Maitreyī
—Transition from philosophy to piety—Hindu asceticism—Professor Huxley's critique of asceticism—Pilgrim's
progress under the religion of Brahma—Investiture
and disciplehood—The life of the householder—The
life of the forest-dweller and wandering ascetic—Ultima
Thule.

THE Veda's conception of the polytheistic gods,
and the relations which the early Hindus have
established with them by means of their songs of

praise and nourishing gifts, are of a spirit very
simple. The temper of these things almost guarantees beforehand equally simple notions about death
and future life. There is a paradise above, conceived
oftenest as a solar paradise, where the gods are having a delightful time. Man would be most happy to
have a share in this delight, like the gods immortal.
Therefore the gods are implored to let come to them
the pious man that has spent his substance freely in
their behalf.[1] Next, this elementary belief is fittingly
padded out with simple rites and ancient legends.
The bodies of the dead are burned and their ashes
are consigned to earth. But this is viewed, symbolic-
ally, merely as an act of preparation—cooking it is
called forthright—for that other life of joy. Arms
and utensils, especially sacrificial utensils, are buried
with the corpse. For the occupations and necessi-
ties of those " who have gone forth " (*preta*), as the
dead are called euphemistically, are the same as upon
the earth, sacrificing included. The righteous fore-
fathers of old who have gone forth in the past—they
have found another good place. Especially Yama,
the first royal man, went forth as a pioneer to the
distant heights in the skies. He searched and found
a way for all his descendants. He went before and
found a dwelling from which no power can debar

[1] Rig-Veda I. 31. 7 ; 91. 1 ; 125. 5, 6 ; 5. 55. 4 ; 63. 2.

mortal man. The Fathers of old have travelled it,
and this path leads every earth-born mortal thither.
There in the midst of highest heaven, in the lap of
the Goddess Dawn, beams unfading light, there
eternal waters flow.   There Yama sits under a tree
of beautiful foliage, engaged in an everlasting bout
in the company of the gods ; there mortals gather
after death at Yama's call to behold Varuna. They
have left all imperfections behind them on returning
to their true home, the rich meadows of which no
one can rob them.   In that place there are no lame
nor crooked of limb; the weak no longer pay tribute
to the strong ; all alike share with Yama and the
gods the feast of the gods.

Underneath the coat of sugar the pill of death is
bitter after all. Fitfully the Vedic Hindu regales
himself with the hope of paradise, but his real crav-
ing is expressed in Vedic literature countless times :
" May we live a hundred autumns, surrounded by
lusty sons! " On the way to Yama the dead must
pass the two broad-nosed, four-eyed dogs, the
speckled and the dark ; according to another turn of
this myth these same dogs, originally sun and moon,[1]
wander among men and pick the daily candidates
that are to go on their last pilgrimage. Soon we
hear of the foot-snare of Yama. Think or do what

[1] See above, p. 105.

you will, death remains uncanny. The prospect of
paradise is marred to some extent by visions of hell,
the inevitable analogical opposite of paradise, that
deep place of bottomless, blind darkness, which in
a later time is fitted out with the usual gruesome
stage-setting in the style of Dante's *Inferno*, or the
wall-paintings in the Campo Santo at Pisa.

From the start there is the idea of retribution. To
Yama's blissful seat only they who have done good
may aspire. We remember the belief that the things
sacrificěd and given the priests (the *ishtāpūrta*) await
in highest heaven the faithful as a sort of twin guardian angels, securing for them bliss. On the other
hand, the oppressors of the Brahmans, "they who
spit upon the Brāhmana sit in the middle of a pool
of blood chewing hair." . . . "The tears which did
roll from the eyes of the oppressed, lamenting Brāhmana, these very ones, O oppressor of Brahmans, the
gods did assign to thee as thy share of water."[1] In
an early version of hell the sage Bhrigu observes
some yelling men who are being cut up and devoured
by other men who also yell: "So they have done to
us in yonder world, so we do to them in return in
this world."[2]

But now the Hindu, subtle and at the same time
naive, given over to rigid schematism and mechan-

[1] Atharva-Veda 5. 19. 3. and 13.
[2] Çatapatha Brāhmana 11. 16. 1.

ical consistency, as all his intellectual history shows, becomes nervous about the permanence of life after death. What if the effect even of his good deeds should not last forever? What if, instead of the hoped-for immortality in yonder world, there be death again? One text fancies a limited immortality which lasts only a hundred years, that is, the ideal length of the life of man upon earth. The treasure of good deeds is after all finite; day and night, or, as we should say, time may exhaust the stock of one's good works. In strict logic that must mean death anew. So we read in the Brāhmaṇa texts of fervent wishes and cunning rites potent to ensure imperishableness of one's good works, and to cut off the possible recurrence of death.[2] There are also performances intended to secure to the deceased ancestors who, for aught one knows, are in the same danger of re-dying, genuine, instead of temporary and conditional immortality.[3] This "death-anew," or "re-death" (*punarmṛtyu*) as the Hindus call it, is an exceedingly characteristic idea, but it is not yet transmigration of souls. As long as its scene is located entirely in the other world, and as long as it is thought possible to avoid or cure it by the ordinary expedients of sacrifice, so long the essential character

---

[1] Çatapatha Brāhmana 10. 1. 5. 4.
[2] Taittirīya Brāhmana 3. 11. 8. 5.
[3] Çatapatha Brāhmana 12. 9. 3. 12.

of that belief is not yet present. But the transition from one to the other was easy. If men can die in heaven there is no way, short of annihilation, to secure peace for anything that started out by being mortal. Next, the notion of " re-death " in the imagined world beyond was after all too shadowy ; it lacked the practical data of experience. It was very natural to transplant the consequences of " re-death " to this earth, the home and hearth of death where men, like fish, die at every wink of the eye. He who must die again comes on to do it on earth where the trick is so well understood—lo and behold, we have the essential of metempsychosis, namely a succession of lives and deaths in the career of one and the same being. I am far from believing that even such smooth reasoning, taken by itself, suffices to account for the presence of this important doctrine in India. The germs of the belief in transmigration are very likely to have filtered into the Brahmanical consciousness from below, from popular sources, possibly from some of the aboriginal, non-Aryan tribes of India. Brahmanical religion has always borrowed immensely from folk beliefs and practices, and has always managed to impart to these borrowings the look of integral Brahmanical doctrine.

Like a will-o'-the-wisp the belief in transmigration [1]

[1] See Alfred Bertholet, *Seelenwanderung* (Nr. 2 of the iii. Series

flares up in many parts of the world. We hear of it among the Egyptians and the Celts, but it has developed most significantly among the Greeks and Hi—dus. Its wide vogue is due to a fusion of some of the simplest observations and reasonings about life and death, such as can scarcely fail to come to the mind of primitive man. It is pure folk-lore. Three suppositions are required for this belief:

First, man has a soul, separate and separable from the body.

Secondly, animals, plants, and even inanimate objects similarly have souls.

Thirdly, all these souls can change their habitations.

The belief that man has a soul depends in the main upon two observations: First, breath of life and its cessation after death. Life's breath is construed by primitive observers as an entity which lives with the living body and leaves it at death. When life's breath departs, the soul departs. Secondly, intercourse of the living with the dead continues in dreams and hallucinations. This shows that the dead after all exist. Primitive man does not recognise illusions.

The belief in animal and plant souls, and even

of *Religionsgeschichtliche Volksbücher*, edited by Professor Friederich Michael Schiele), Halle a. S. 1904.

souls of inanimate objects (fetish), is based upon
the same sort of simple logic. Animals have both
life's breath and some measure of reason. Nomads,
cattle-raisers, hunters, inhabitants of forest and sea-
coast are thrown into intimate intercourse, each with
particular classes of animals whose mental resources
are not only obvious, but often clash with man's
interests. Clear up into the high literature of beast
fable and fairy-tale survives the folk's very real
belief in reasoning, soul-inhabited animals: see Rey-
nard the Fox and Bre'r Rabbit. Primitive man, too,
in the search after his own origin has often blun-
dered into the notion that man is descended from
one or the other animal. This has given rise to the
very important religious, political, and economic
institutions known as Totemism.

As regards plants, the Hindu Law-Book of Manu
forbids the chewing of red rosin, doubtless because
it looks like coagulated blood, and blood must not
be drunk.[1] The tree is supposed to be alive. The
weird twilight shapes of trees and plants, the sough
of the wind in the leaves of the forest-trees again
suggest life in the vegetable kingdom.

As regards inanimate things, we need but remember the child's relation to its doll, or, that children
punish with their own oft-tasted penalties the stick

[1] See von Negelein, *Archiv für Religionswissenschaft*, vi., 246.

over which they stumble. In brief, the nearer or
remoter analogies of human life which pervade, or
seem to pervade all objects in nature present themselves to early man as guarantees or suggestions of
universal animation, of souls present in every shapen
thing.

And now the passage of these souls from one kind
of receptacle to another, from man to man, from
man to animal, plant, or stock, or stone, follows
inevitably. The records of primitive beliefs are full
of it. I will merely remind you of the belief in wer-
wolves as one instance of this kind. In the final
outcome of all these notions some peoples, eager to
account for the destiny of man after death, have
assumed a chain of variegated existences. And with
this goes very generally some notion of evolution
forward or backward. The character of the creature
in a certain given existence controls the degree of
the next existence. This last bit of logic has
flowered out in India as the important doctrine of
karma or " deed." [1]

As far as India is concerned one thing is certain :
real metempsychosis does not enter into the higher
thought of India, or, at least, is not stated unmistakably until we come to the Upanishads. When,
however, this belief has finally taken shape we find in

[1] See below p. 259.

17

it the following established items of faith: Every
living creature is reborn in some organic shape;
every living creature had a previous existence; and
every living creature is again and again the prey of
death, until in some life all desire and all activity as
the outcome of desire shall have been laid aside.
This is the Hindu salvation, namely, absolute resig-
nation of the finite, futile, illusory world; cessation
of the will to live, and the act of living. This of
itself produces union with Brahma. Not until mortal man has cast off every desire of his heart does he
enter immortal into Brahma. We have now arrived
at the thought or the position of the Upanishads, the
last in the long line of Vedic texts. Like all Vedic
thought, the thought of the Upanishads is not systematic, but tentative, fanciful, and even romantic. It
feels its way through misty, wavering, sometimes
conflicting beginnings. The more rigid conclusions
come later on in one or the other of the so-called
systems of Hindu philosophy.

Still even in the Upanishads so important a doctrine must be established on reason. There are two
questions to be asked. First, why must the soul
wander from life to life; secondly, why does its habi-
tation differ from life to life, liable to reincarnation:
at one time as an animal high or low; at another as
a human being of various degrees; and at yet an-

other even as a god ? For our convenience we may answer the second question first. The celebrated Law-Book of Manu, at a time when this doctrine has become cut and dried, teaches that a Brahman priest who steals the substance which has been entrusted to him for sacrifice to the gods will in his next existence become a vulture or a crow. [1] Why ? Because the vulture and the crow make their living by stealing food. Briefly, man is what he does.

Note the superb moral possibilities of this teaching. This is the well-known doctrine of *karma*, or " deed," now famous wherever men are interested in the evolution of the human mind. Deed and the will, or " desire," as the Hindus call it, back of the deed, are essentially one and the same thing. On desire man's nature is founded ; as his desires so are his endeavors, as his endeavors so are his deeds. By his deeds the character of his next birth in the round of existences is regulated, for he is himself the sum of his own deeds. If his *karma* in a given life has accumulated for him a good balance, as it were, the next life will be delightful and noble ; conversely, if his life is evil, the next birth will be, consequently, as a low and degraded being. Life is character—character inherited and inherent from previous existence, and character modelled and shaped by the deeds of

[1] Manu 11. 25.

the present existence.   Now we may answer the first
question, namely, Why must the soul wander at all?
The answer is :   No deed leads the way to salvation,
to release from life and union with Brahma.   Aye, to
be sure, as the fragrance of a tree in blossom so the
fragrance of a good deed is wafted afar, saith the
Chāndogya Upanishad.[1]   But even the best deed is
a thing from its very nature limited and vitiated by
the finite. It rewards itself, it punishes itself, according to a process of automatic psychic evolution, but
the fruit of the finite can itself be only finite :

"Yājnavalkya," says Ārtabhāga in the "Great Forest
Upanishad,"[2] " if, after the death of this man, his
speech goes into fire, his breath into wind, his eye into
the sun, his mind into the moon, his ear into the directions of space, his body into the earth, his self (*ātman*)
into ether, the hair of his body into plants, the hair
of his head into trees, his blood and semen into water,
—what then becomes of the man?"   Then spake
Yājnavalkya: "Take me by the hand, my dear!
Ārtabhāga, we two must come to an understanding
about this privately, not here among people."   And
they went out and consulted.   And what they said
was DEED (*karma*), and what they praised was DEED :
'Verily, one becomes good through good deed, evil
through evil deed."

[1] 5. 10. 9.

[2] Brihadāranyaka Upanishad 3. 2. 13.

Later in the same tract[1] Yājnavalkya describes the departure of the soul from the body and its consequences to man: "Then his knowledge and his works and his previous experience take him by the hand. As a caterpillar which has wriggled to the tip of a blade of grass draws itself over to (a new blade), so does this man, after he has put aside his body, draw himself over to a new existence. . . Now verily they say: 'Man is altogether desire (*kāma*); as is his desire so is his insight (*kratu*); as is his insight so is his deed (*karma*); as is his deed so is his destiny.'"

More than one Western reader, when he ponders the doctrine of transmigration as rooted in desire and deed, is likely to ask the question why the Hindus did not rest content with its outcome. The bulk of their spiritual energy in Brahmanism, as well as in Buddhism and the other Hindu sects, is expended in the effort to break the chain that ties man to existence. Why is this so? The Western man, if I gauge him aright, is willing to tarry in the life garden of will, desire, and deed, plucking its fruits and flowers at the risk of an occasional prick from its thorns, or sting from its noxious insects. We want more life, fuller life. Here are some of the points connected with transmigration that are naturally sympathetic to Western minds:

[1] Brihadāranyaka Upanishad 4. 4. 3; *see also* Brahma Upanishad, chapter the first.

1. Love of life, and abhorrence of annihilation: transmigration ensures life in some form for ever and ever.

2. The twin ghosts of fatalism and predestination are laid. Where will and deed, with character as their result, rule every destiny, nothing is accidental, nothing is pre-determined. Man himself, free from outside interference, is the arbiter of his own destiny.

3. It involves the perfection of retribution: reward and punishment adjust themselves automatically and organically to virtue and vice. It opens wide the door of hope to the lowly and oppressed, and checks the excesses of the cruel mighty. Byron's despairing,

> " Methinks we have sinned in some old world
> And this is Hell,"

loses its sting. It is mere justice. But it is the justice that knows how to reward merit just as unerringly, as it knows how to punish sin inexorably. There is no human being so hedged in by calamity, vice, and degradation, but what he or she may start on the upward road by some act of determination for good. If the wish, " Grant me my heaven now," fails of fulfilment, who knows that it may not be fulfilled in the train of heroic effort?

And yet the deep-seated instinct of life which makes men all over the earth, India included, wail

their dead, goes hand in hand in all higher forms of
Hindu religion with the apparently sincere expression of a desire to be released from life.   Pessimism,
at first negative, in the end positive and profound,
becomes the ruling theory of Hindu life.   With all the
attractions, fascinations, and beauties of life, life is
felt to be a fetter, or a knot which ties the heart to
the world of sense ; and release (*moksha*) from the
everlasting round of lives (*samsāra*) is the Hindu
salvation (*nirvāna*).   Buddhism later on expresses
the urgent need of salvation from existence in its
well-known fourfold doctrine of suffering.   Its first
clause establishes the truth of suffering :   Birth is
suffering ; age is suffering ; disease is suffering ; union
with what is not loved is suffering ; separation from
what is loved is suffering.   The conviction that all
life is futile is expressed hardly less distinctly in the
Great Forest Upanishad (3. 5. 2), where hunger and
thirst, woe and delusion, age and death, desire for
children, and desire for possessions are lumped alike
as the evils and vanities of life, before the highest
knowledge has been attained.[1]   Anyhow, all the
principal Hindu systems of religion and philosophy

[1] " How many births are past, I cannot tell ;
  How many yet to come, no man can say :
  But this alone I know, and know full well,
  That pain and grief embitter all the way."
(South-Indian Folk-song, quoted in the Rev. Dr. John Morrison's
New Ideas in India, p. 213.)

start out with the assurance that the world is full of suffering, and that is their particular business to account for it and to remove it.

We must not forget that the perpetual decay and death and replacement which is the gist of human life when looked at purely from the outside is not redeemed in India by any theory, or instinctive faith in general advancement. There is in all Hindu thought no expression of hope for the race, no theory of betterment all along the line. Each individual must attend to his own uplifting that is to free him from a world whose worthlessness is condemned in unmeasured terms. Admitting that this is to no small extent mere theory; that the average Hindu worries along, sustained by life, hope, sunshine, and what not, whence the theory?

The question has frequently been put point blank: How did Hindu pessimism originate? I believe that the answer, or at least a partial answer, may be made with some degree of certainty, to wit: India herself, through her climate, her nature, and her economic conditions, furnishes reasonable ground for pessimism. As regards economic conditions political economists say that the value of human life in any country may be estimated by the average wage of its earners. A low caste servant may to-day be engaged for a wage of five cents a day out of which he must, owing to caste laws, find his own keep, and possibly that of a family besides. India's nature is more malignant than that of any other civilised country. The floods of great rivers devastate at times entire districts; per contra, when the rains are withheld at the time of the capricious monsoons, famine with plague or cholera in its wake, decimate the population. The tribe of venomous serpents and the blood-lust of the tiger claim their regular quota of victims.

Our first acquaintance with the Aryan Hindus in the hymns of the Veda shows them to us a sturdy, life-loving people on the banks, or in the region of the river Indus, the land of the five streams, the modern Punjab in Northwestern India. That country they had conquered, fresh from the highlands that separate India from Iran. By successive contests, hinted at in a very interesting legend of the Brāhmana texts [1] they advanced eastward, until they had overrun the plain of the Ganges—the hottest civilised land on the face of the earth. This is the land of Hindu theosophy, the land of the Upanishads, the land where Buddha preached, some centuries after the earliest Upanishads. Buddha's most famous sermon was delivered at Benares, in the very centre of the plain of the Ganges. There

[1] Catapatha Brāhmana 1. 4. 1. 10–18.

in.the land of Bengal, if anywhere on the face of the
civilised earth, the doubts and misgivings that beset
human life at its best might permanently harden into
the belief that life is a sorry affair. Hindu literature
that comes from these lands shows us that the
Aryans did not succumb to this change, for they
remain a great and remarkable people. But this
habitat of theirs unquestionably left an indelible
impression on their character. The mental subtle-
ness of the race did not perish, but their bodies
suffered ; hypochondria, melancholia, dyspepsia—
call it what we may—conquered the conquering
Aryan, whose stock was no doubt the product of a
more northerly and invigorating climate.

Now it is time to remember once more that the
conception of the One True Being—let us now call
it Brahma—had risen to a considerable height, apparently long before the doctrine of transmigration
had taken hold of the Hindu mind, and established
in it the theory of despair of the world. Even aside
from such a theory it is natural for the mind of man
in every clime and time to evolve some great power
that is behind the phenomena of the world, to establish to its own satisfaction some sort of perfect
principle that is underneath this obviously imperfect
world, and then to long for some kind of association
with that power or principle. So teach us all higher

religions and religious philosophies. Without doubt the Hindus did this before pessimism and independently of pessimism. But when pessimism began to taint the Hindu view of life, then the eternal all-force, the root of all, the One True and Perfect Thing offered the only logical escape from the evils of existence.

The theory of the Brahma and the theory of transmigration united like the two branches of a river. The wandering of the soul through the realms governed by death must be the consequence of its separation from Brahma. As long as lasts the will to live this life of death, as long as this will means finite desires and finite deed, so long the soul remains separate from Brahma in the chain of successive lives and deaths, each new life shaped by the *karma* of the preceding life. Escape from this chain can be accomplished only by union with the Single True Being, the Brahma.

Hinduism has again in this matter taken a remarkable turn, if we test it by the normal temper of the Western mind. It is a kind of dualistic pessimism, in which the good that is in the world as well as the evil that is there are both made to emphasise the evil. It is a pessimism that is reached through both avenues ; the avenue of evil, because it is evil ; and the avenue of good, because it suggests by its very

terms the existence of evil. We Westerners have
learned one way or another to endure this naughty
world fairly well. But when it becomes too bad we
are apt to remember that the refuge is with the
Omnipotent Power. That is the silver lining to the
cloud of human existence. The Hindu mind turns
this the other way; the silvery sheen of Brahma has
a cloud lining. The conception of this One True
Being, out of which flow all visible things, might
have been an anchor of strength and a head-spring
of hope and joy for the Hindus. A palpably possible consequence of their thought is, that all men
have the divine or Brahmic spark, that all are micro-
cosms, flung off—for some reason—by that superb
macrocosm, the Brahma. If so, then individual
human existence must be based upon truth and
wholesomeness, no less than the Universal Brahma.
Not so did the Hindus proceed. They lavish upon
the Brahma all imaginable attributes of perfection, and then proceed to apply the same standard
to this world: of course they find it by contrast a
very sorry affair. The world ceases to be a desirable
home in which one may live, sustained perhaps by
the hope of better things to come, because it is
measured by the standard of Brahma and found
wanting. When the Brahma is praised, that Brahma
which is lifted above hunger and thirst, above grief

and worry, above old age, decay, and death, the persistent personal application is, that this world of
creatures is full of hunger, thirst, grief, worry, old
age, decay, and death.

There is yet one consequence to be drawn. The
question is asked, as it must be: "What is the cure
for desire, the thirst for life and its contents? How
cut the fetter, or the knot of adhesion to the illusory
world? How get rid of the will to live?" The
answer is, through knowledge. Knowledge, or perhaps it would be better to say intuition, of the
unity of the individual self with the great True One ;
and the recognition, ever present, of the divided, distracted, illusory nature of everything finite: When
a mortal has recognised Brahma, feeling, "He is
myself," how can he longer desire and cling to
bodily life? This is the culminating thought of the
Upanishads and the Veda, expressed in the solemn
three words *tat tvam asi*, "Thou art That." That
is to say, the essence of man is itself Brahma. The
wise man when once he has seen That (*tad apaçyat*),
becomes That (*tad abhavat*), because in truth he
always was and is That (*tad āsīt*).[1] Thus the final
attainment of man is this knowledge; it is the
"works" of the Jew, and the "faith" of the
Christian—salvation by the complete ascendency

[1] See Vājasaneyi Samhitā (Tadeva Upanishad), 32. 12.

of the divine in one's self, and the consequent submergence of all that is temporal and illusory.

It is time now that we return to the last question which I propounded for to-day's lecture. How did the *brahma*, the One, the Universal spirit, finally shape himself from out of the mass of ideas whose constant drift was in the direction of oneness, or, as we may finally call it, monistic pantheism? One of the main circumstances of the higher religious thought of the time just preceding the Upanishads was a strong monotheistic tendency which seemed to develop simultaneously and peacefully along with the monistic ideas, such as the "That," the "Only," the "Being."

In the Upanishads monotheism is practically at an end, whereas the attempts to designate the abstract conceptions just mentioned emerge from the stage of tremulous venture to confident and familiar statement. Yet they are not any one of them the final name of the Universal Being. Even the Upanishad mind seems to prefer something more tangible and suggestive, something that after all has attributes.

In the seething caldron of the earlier speculation there occur yet two other conceptions which have become pretty well crystallised even before the time of the Upanishads. The first of these is the con-

ception of the *ātman*, which means first "breath,"
and then "self." As far as the early poetry is concerned there is not the least doubt about the primary
meaning of *ātman*.[1] It is familiarly correlated with
wind, "the breath of the gods."[2] The *ātman* or
soul of man after death returns to mingle with the
wind from which it is supposed to have come.[3] The
later Veda abounds in crude and fanciful psycho-
physical observations in which the parts and functions of the human body, the little cosmos, are
correlated more or less skilfully with the phenomena
of the outer world, the big cosmos. An important
thought of this sort is, that the human body is per-
vaded by plural breaths, *prānas* or *ātmans;* these
vivify the body, and are the essential part, the *ego*,
of the living individual. Several of the older Upanishads contain a fable, resembling the Latin fable of
"the belly and the members." The vital powers
are quarrelling among themselves for supremacy.
They bring their case before Prajāpati, "the lord of
creatures." Prajāpati advises them to leave the body
one by one and to observe which loss affects it
most. The voice, the eye, the ear, the mind de-

[1] For the meaning of *tman*, the reduced stem of the same word in
the pronominal sense of "self," see the author in *American Journal
of Philology*, xvi., p. 421.
[2] Rig-Veda 7. 87. 2 ; 10. 168. 4.
[3] *Ibid.*, 10. 16. 3 ; 90. 13 ; 92. 13.

parted, discommoding the body quite a good deal.
But when the breath was on the point of departing,
"just as the proud steed from the Indus would pull
and tear the pegs of his tether, so it pulled and tore
the other vital powers." And they yielded the palm
to the *ātman*. Hence a text declares: "From the
ātman all the members spring into existence. Of
all things that come into existence the *ātman* is the
first."

The *ātmans*, or breaths, are finally conceived as
coming from a single *ātman*, the universal breath,
or self, or *ego*. A Brāhmana text declares: "Ten
(kinds of) breath dwell in man ; the universal *ātman*
is the eleventh : all the breaths are contained in
him." That is, the *ātman*, after its supreme place in
the own self has been permanently fixed, is trans-
ferred on exactly the same terms to the universe
outside of man. The *ātman*, the lord of breaths, is
at the same time the lord of the gods, the creator of
all beings ; all the worlds are an emanation of his
great universal self : finally the *ātman* is the all.

It is easy to see that with all the refinement of
the term *ātman* in its final outcome, it certainly has
a strong physical touch, at least in the beginning of
its use. The final shaping of the idea consisted in
associating, or rather fusing, with this *ātman* another
conception, coming from a totally different quarter,

namely, the olden Vedic sphere of devotion, prayer, holy performance, in fact religion in general. Even in the Vedic hymns, as we have seen, the epithet "Goddess" is freely given to the numerous names for prayer, devotion, religious emotion, and kindred ideas. Unquestionably the *sāvitrī* stanza owes its puzzlingly paramount position in Hindu religion to the same estimate of devotion as a thing essentially divine.[1] We have also made acquaintance with a symbolic "Lord of Prayer," Brihaspati, an important, but not lasting attempt to pour the sacred function of the poets and priests into the mould of a personal god. He marks one of those false starts towards personal monotheism in which the later Veda abounds. More and more the sacred word, the constant companion of the sacrifice, is felt to be a kind of uplifting spiritual essence. The sacred word is *brahma*. Starting as prayer,[2] charm, sacred formula, religious act, it becomes the symbol of holy thought and holy utterance (λόγος), the outpouring of the soul in its highest longings. It is the best wish of a spiritually

[1] See above, p. 202.

[2] Professor Oldenberg regards " zauberfluidum " as the original meaning of *brahma*. But does " magic essence " really explain, and does it not itself stand in need of explanation ? Anyway it seems to me that this distinguished scholar's present sympathy with what may be called ethnological explanations of religious phenomena, that is the theory that such phenomena must necessarily begin somewhere in the lowest bathos of savage folk belief, is leading him on a trail farther than that trodden by this word.

18

minded and gifted people that becomes for a while personal gôd, and at last the divine essence of the universe. The conception is intellectually not as subtle and abstract as the monistic philosophical conception of "That Only True Being," which comes entirely from the head. But from the point of view of heart-felt emotion it is the most exalted divine conception of gentile folk. Such is *the brahma*, used in the neuter gender, not yet the masculine God Brahma who, after a renewed personification is placed at the head of the later Hindu so-called trinity, Brahma, Vishnu, and Çiva : "The *brahma* is the word, the truth in the word is *brahma*. Through *brahma* heaven and earth are held together."

The two conceptions of *ātman* and *brahma*, in their origin, respectively, the physical and spiritual essences of the universe, are fused into one conception. They are used in general as synonyms. Still there is a tendency to use *brahma*, " Holy Thought," as the designation of the universal principle in the outer world ; *ātman*, " Self," as the same principle in the inner life of man. The conviction that the *brahma* without and the *ātman* within are one and the same, that is the real religion of the Upanishads. The power which operates in the universe, creating, sustaining, and destroying, the power behind this imperfect world that perchance moves on to some

final development ; the power that manifests itself in
every living thing ;—this eternal power is identical
with our own innermost and truest self, equally
imperishable when stripped of all its external and
accidental circumstances. This conviction is em-
balmed in the famous words, *tat tvam asi,* "Thou
art That," or *aham brahma asmi,* "I am the
Brahma." These are the slogans of higher religious
thought ; and they contain the corollary that the
world of things which we see in space, as we ideally
assume it to be with our eyes and bodies, themselves
phenomena, are mere shadows cast by the one truth
—the innermost Personal Self identical with the
outer Universal Self, the *brahma-ātman.*[1]

Now we have seen that our empirical knowledge
which shows us a manifold variegated world where in
truth there is only *brahma,* and a body where there
is in truth only *ātman,* or the *brahma* in ourselves,
that all that is mere ignorance, distraction, or illusion.
The things that are unfolded before our eyes in space,
those things to which we ourselves belong with our
ponderable bodies, are not true entities, they are not

[1] The Catholic mystic, Johannes Scheffler, called Angelus Silesius
(born 1624), arrives at the same end in a stanza of his collection of
poems called *Cherubinischer Wandersmann :*

> " Ich bin so gross wie Gott,
> Er ist wie ich so klein ;
> Ich kann nicht unter ihm,
> Er über mich nicht sein."

the *ātman*. As long as this is not recognised, the Hindus say there is *avidyā* "ignorance," or, more literally and philosophically "nescience." Or they say that there is *māyā* "illusion." All else aside from this single truth is a mere mirage in the desert, and is so far as it must after all have some kind of a connection with Brahma, have some reality in Brahma, it is no more real than the reflection of the real moon which we see trembling on the ripple of the waters. Even the very conception of nescience or illusion is, of course, not real, because it can be annihilated, and whatever is temporary is not real. What induced the time-less, space-less, and cause-less Brahma to enter upon the escapade of this phenomenal world of time, space, and causality, the Hindu thinkers cannot tell us. Their mythology is full of crude ideas of the primitive being's loneliness and desire to multiply, but these ideas belong to the lower forms of their religion ; they are not entertained by their philosophers. This is the point where Hinduism like every system of idealistic philosophy breaks down. Plato's τὸ ὄντως ὄν ; the *ens realissimum;* Kant's *ding an sich;* the Upanishads' "That only True" are all very well, but the world of phenomena to explain that—aye there 's the rub. This pesky world of plural things, full of irrational quantities—why does it exist, and is it not pounding along toward some end that will show a uniting principle? With that kind of suggestion the Hindu will have nothing to do. Entranced by the absolute reality of the one Brahma he wafts away the world of experience as a conjurer an optical delusion.

Into the maze of difficulties and inconsistencies which opens out here we need not go. The manifold modifications, adjustments, and the trimming down of the main thought which the Upanishads are driven to undertake belong to philosophy rather than religion. According to the Upanishads' own definition of the *ātman*, everything that these works undertake to say about anything other than the *ātman* is mere figure of speech, and every definition of the *ātman* itself is also figure of speech. Every definition is necessarily stopped by the words: "No, No" (*na neti*). The Brahma has no attributes (*nirguna*). Yea, the Hindu when in the proper mood, advancing straight to the last consequence, looking neither to the right nor to the left, denies the possibility of knowing Brahma altogether. Tremendous paradox this, considering all depends upon the intuition of this very conception. In a conversation with his wife Maitreyī[1] the great thinker Yājnavalkya asserts that there is no consciousness after death, because there must be two in order that one should see

[1] Brihadāranyaka Upanishad 2. 4. 12 *ff.*

the other, smell, hear, address, understand, recognise the other. "But if one has himself become *Ātman* (that is, "Self") by means of what and whom should he then see? By means of what and whom should he then smell, hear, address, understand, recognise?" In brief and dry language, being himself the subject, and there being no object, there is no cognition nor consciousness.

Emerson's keen and terse poem on the Brahma in which the Brahma itself speaks, approaches this idea of absolute unity. But the chilly sombre theme is made warm and glowing in these lines which may be counted among the best in the English language:

> If the red slayer think he slays,
>   Or if the slain think he is slain,
> They know not well the subtle ways
>   I keep, and pass, and turn again.
>
> Far and forgot to me is near,
>   Shadow and sunlight are the same,
> The vanished gods to me appear,
>   And one to me are shame and fame.
>
> They reckon ill who leave me out;
>   When me they fly I am the wings;
> I am the doubter and the doubt.
>   And I the hymn the Brahmin sings.
>
> The strong gods pine for my abode
>   And pine in vain, the Sacred Seven;
> But thou meek lover of the good!
>   Find me, and turn thy back on heaven.

But we are concerned with the value of the Upanishads as religion, in a world which for practical purposes must be admitted to be real, for man who for practical purposes must be admitted to be real. The Çvetāçvatara Upanishad starts out with the old question :

Whence are we born ? Whereby do we live, and whither do we go ? O ye who know Brahma, tell us at whose command we abide here, whether in pain or in pleasure ? Should Time, or nature, or necessity, or chance, or the elements be considered as the cause, or he who is called Purusha, that is, the Supreme Spirit ?

The Upanishads answer for practical purposes : The Supreme Spirit that is alike in the universe and in man—that is the essence of all. It is Being, without a second, without beginning and without end, without limitations of any kind. Whatever there is, or seems to be, mind and matter, nature and man, is one substance only, namely, Brahma. The same Yājnavalkya, whose desperately rationalistic answer to his wife Maitreyī we have just heard, takes also a more human view of the Ātman. This is told in the frame of a quaint little story, as follows [1] :

Yājnavalkya had two wives, Maitreyī and Kātyāyanī. Of these two Maitreyī knew how to discourse about the

[1] Brihadāranyaka Upanishad 2. 4 and 4. 5.

brahma ; Kātyāyanī, on the other hand, knew only what women are supposed to understand. Now Yājnavalkya desired to change his life of householder to that of religious hermit.

"Maitreyī," says he, "I shall now retire from the condition of householder, and as a preliminary divide my goods between thee and Kātyāyanī." Then spake Maitreyī : " If, O lord, this whole earth with all its wealth belonged to me, would I then become immortal, or not ? " " By no means," replies Yājnavalkya. " Only like the life of the rich would thy life be ; wealth does not carry with it the expectation of immortality." Then replied Maitreyī : " That through which I do not become immortal, what good is that to me ? Expound to me rather thy knowledge." Then Yājnavalkya : "Truly thou wast previously dear to us, beloved lady, and now thou hast increased our love. Well then, I shall expound it to thee ; attend then, to what I say : All things of the world, and every relation in the world are dear to us not because of their own value, but because of the *ātman,* their true essence. Wife, husband, sons, wealth ; the high stations of priest and warrior ; the worlds, the gods, the Veda, and the sacrifice are dear to us not because of their own value, but because of the *ātman,* their true essence. As one grasps the tones of an instrument with the instrument itself so are grasped all things when the *ātman* is grasped. Truly he that hath seen, heard, recognised, and understood the *ātman* he knows the whole world." [1]

We may be sure that Yājnavalkya does not really intend to expound to his beloved Maitreyī the ex-

[1] *Cf. Rāmakrishna, His Life and Sayings,* p. 135 (number 161).

tremes of super-sensual rationalism. In effect he
expresses the ideal of union with the supreme being,
the ultimate endeavor of all religions that have
evolved a supreme being worth uniting with. At
a later period there comes out of the permanently
untenable, cool intellectualism of the Upanishads
the religion of the Bhāktas or "pious devotees."
The destiny of Upanishad thought is, after all, an
acute and mystic monotheism, very like the mysti-
cism of those Christian " friends of god," John Tauler
and Thomas à Kempis. By knowledge they discover the Supreme Intelligence and perceive its
essence ; by devotion (*bhakti*) they feel the sweet-
ness of the Supreme Being and reciprocate its loving
intent. So the Bhagavadgītā, the " Song of the Celestial," can finally make the Supreme Being say of the
pious man: "Through love he recognises me in
truth, my greatness and my essence. He that loves
me is not lost." It comes to this finally, that knowledge of the Supreme is but a preparation for what
we call love of God. In the words of the modern
Bengāli Saint and Ascetic Rāmakrishna : " The
Knowledge of God may be likened to a man, while
the Love of God is like a woman. Knowledge has
entry only up to the outer rooms of God, but no
one can enter into the inner mysteries of God save
a lover, for a woman has access even to the privacy

of the Almighty."[1]   And finally the same thinker
arrives at the last possible conclusion : " Knowledge
and love of God are ultimately one and the same.
There is no difference between pure knowledge and
pure love." We might have predicted the same
result. To a religion which strives with all its might
to know the truth, truth's sister, love, does not long
remain a stranger.

Yājnavalkya, as we have seen, abandons his wives
and goes to live in the forest. Such " Forest-
Hermits " (ὑλόβιοι) must have been common in
India several centuries before Christ.   Buddha criti-
cises them, and declares himself as against their
ascetic life and practices as a hindrance rather than
a help to a life of perfect freedom from passions and
desires, a life of true emancipation. He himself
advocates moderation in all things, salvation included.   He prefers the " middle of the road," as
both he and we say (the *media via*, or *madhyama-
mārga*).   About 300 B.C. a clever Greek by the name
of Megasthenes was the ambassador of the Græco-
Persian king Seleukos at the court of Chandragupta
in the city of Pātaliputra (311–302 B.C).   Chandragupta—Sandrakottos or Sandrokyptos as the Greeks
called him—had succeeded, after the death of Alexander the Great, in founding the great Indian empire

[1] *Rāmakrishna, His Life and Sayings*, p. 138 (number 172).

of the Maurya dynasty, the largest empire known up to that time in India. Megasthenes wrote a work called *Indica* which contains much important information about the India of his day. He tells that these ascetics were indifferent to the good or evil that happens to man ; that all being, in their opinion, is dreamlike illusion ; that they regard the world as created and perishable ; and believe that God who has created it pervades it completely. Considering the source, this is an uncommonly good description of the pessimistic pantheism of the Upanishads. Alexander the Great himself was much impressed with these " Sages of the Forest." He sent one Onesikritos to talk with them. After having been laughed at by the ascetics for his full dress of mantle, hat, and boots, and told to lie naked upon the stones if he would learn from them, he was finally initiated into the Hindu idea, to wit, that the best doctrine is that which removes not only sorrow but also joy from the soul of man.

Professor Huxley in his *Evolution and Ethics* (p. 65) has subjected the Hindu ideal to severe criticism. According to him the *summum bonum* of the Hindu is a state of impassive quasi-somnambulism which but for its acknowledged holiness might run the risk of being confounded with idiocy. It leads to the abandonment of property, social ties, family affections, and common companionship, until all that remains of a man is the impassive attenuated mendicant monk, self-hypnotised into cataleptic trances which the deluded mystic takes for foretastes of final union with Brahma. Professor Huxley has in mind the extreme case of Yogin of the later time, who confounds hocus-pocus and humbug with religion. As a matter of fact the Upanishad religion is a religion of perfect freedom, and equally as a matter of fact the religious of the Upanishads do find it advisable as a rule to retire from active life after having done their duty in active life.

Yājnavalkya's step marks not only the new order of thought but also the new order of life which the religion of the *ātman-brahma* imposes upon India. In fact we may say that henceforth India leads a double life. The first is the life of every day. The fragile human creature enters through the mother's womb, where it has been protected by the pious prayers and ceremonies of its parents, into the bewildering sunshine of this world. If it only knew it, it would be glad that the *karma* of its former existence entitles its soul in the present existence to the shelter of a human body, howsoever lowly. Worse might have happened in the hazard of the lottery of transmigration. Birth means that the soul in question has not yet joined Brahma. He who has not

done so, alas, is born again as worm or as fly ; as fish
or as fowl ; as lion or as boar ; as bull or as tiger, or
man ; or as something else—any old thing as we
might say—in this place or in that place, according
to the quality of his works, and the degree of his
knowledge, that is in accordance with the doctrine
of *karma.*[1]   Thanks to the past the present is secure :
worse might have happened than to pass through
the temporary shelter of a human mother's body
into the more enduring shelter of the mother's love.
The Hindu mother, like any other mother, rejoices
in her child, especially if he is a boy, and asks no
questions about his ultimate cosmic destiny.   Father
and mother now bend every energy to raise the child
so that he may become an honored member of the
Brahmanical community, beloved alike of god and
man.   The Hindu books of Rules of Home Life, the
so-called Grihyasūtras,[2] tell a touching story of the
pious care with which the child is piloted through
infancy.   Indeed the life of the Brahmanical Hindu
is sacramental throughout.   Every important phase
of his life has its own sacraments.   The most important of them are the investiture by his teacher
with the sacred cord, and his marriage.

This investiture is looked upon as a spiritual

[1] Kāushītaki Upanishad 1. 2.
[2] See above, p. 41.

second birth, or regeneration. The little mortal becomes a man in a higher sense, because his teacher teaches him the Veda, syllable by syllable, word by word, stanza by stanza. During the period of his disciplehood he is the devoted servant of his teacher who, throughout Hindu tradition, is regarded as even better entitled to respect than his own parents. No matter how rich and powerful his own family, he now lives obedient to his teacher, taking care of his wants to the point of gathering his fire-wood and begging for him in the village, humble and chaste in his own life. In return he obtains from his teacher the sacred knowledge, the Veda. Especially, the sacrosanct Sāvitrī, that famous brief stanza[1] which at an early time carries within it the presentiment of the deep theosophy that is to come, by placing in the relation of cause and effect the physical and spiritual essences of the universe:

> "That lovely glory of Savitar,
> The heavenly god, we contemplate :
> Our pious thoughts he shall promote."

After he has absolved the study of the Veda he becomes a full-grown man. The teacher, according to the beautiful account of the Taittirīya Upanishad (i. 11), dismisses his pupil with the following last

[1] Rig-Veda 3. 62. 10 ; see above, p. 86.

injunction: "Tell the truth; do your duty, do not neglect the study of the Veda! After having given to your teacher your gift of love, see to it that the thread of your race be not cut off! Do not neglect truth, duty, health, property, and the study of the Veda! Honor your mother as a god! Honor your father as a god! Honor your teacher as a god! Honor your guest as a god! Live an irreproachable life; honor your superior; give alms in true spirit! When in doubt follow the judgment of Brahmans of tried authority!"

Then he passes into the life stage of full-grown man, husband and householder (*grhastha*). His great duties are now worship and sacrifice to the gods,—and the begetting of sons. The latter are of great importance, because they carry on through unbroken generations the cult of the Manes or Fathers who, in a vaguely inconsistent way, are still carrying on a happy life in the abodes of the blessed—between transmigrations we must suppose. This as reward for their supposedly very pious lives.

It is at the end of this stage that we may suppose Yājnavalkya takes leave of his beloved Maitreyī. The curtain now drops on the scene of all temporal interests: wife, children, home, and property. It is a curious fact that in theory at least the higher religion of the Upanishad begins where the religions of other peoples are content to conclude their offices. Having disciplined the young Brahman ; having taught him how to live an orderly, god-fearing, god-protected life; having secured safe continuation of his race through pious sons; and having finally gained his admission to the heavenly home of the blessed Fathers—what more is needed?

Not so the Hindu. Over this pigmy religion which is engaged only with the needs of the ponderable, perishable man, towers as a giant the grandiose conception, than which, in its way, no higher is possible, that the True in man is in fact the One True in all the Universe. There is one eternal truth: of this we ourselves are part. The distracting, misleading, adhesion, cemented by every sense, to a divided individual existence in a world of illusory phenomena, come no one knows whence, but none the less certainly false, requires time and patience to undo. The Hindu theory assumes four stages or *āçramas* (literally, "hermitages") in the life of man after his rebirth at the investiture. The first two stages, as we have seen, are disciplehood and householdership. Then come the two stages of Forest-dweller, or Hermit, and Wandering Ascetic. In the hermit stage he simply lives in the forest, and may yet keep up some connection with wife and children, and continue his sacred practices. But in the last stage all worldly interest is abandoned, every fetter of affection, desire, passion is sundered. There is no fixed abode, he lives as it happens, subsists as he may, indifferent to all but the realisation that he is the *brahma*. This realisation of itself means the destruction of nescience: with it the phantom world of sorrow and joy sinks out of sight. The soul knowing at last that it is *brahma*, namely truth, sunders the chain that holds it captive through transmigration to the world, namely illusion. This is the salvation of the Hindu, namely the perfect knowledge that the soul of man that dwells in him is the unpolluted, not to be polluted, serene, holy, eternal, blissful, divine self—the *ātman*, or *brahma*. The realisation of this truth, unhindered by any other desire, that is all that is needed; than it nothing else whatsoever can have anything more than temporary importance.

INDEX

A

Aborigines of India, 24, 175
Abstract gods, 96, 109, 131, 135, 191, 242
Açoka or Piyadassi, Buddhist Emperor, 19, 53
Açvamedha, "horse-sacrifice" 213, 216
Açvins, or Dioscuri, 46, 90 *ff.,* 94, 110, 112 *ff.,* 141, 160, 167, 172
Aditi, 130 *ff.*
Ādityas, 78, 92, 120, 129 *ff.,* 153; meaning of the word, 131
Agni and Soma, 78
Agni, "God Fire," 78, 87, 89, 91, 92, 110, 127, 156 *ff.,* 244; son of Ushas (Dawn), 73, 160; his descent from heaven (lightning), 165; produced by friction, 139, 158; progenitor of men (Āyu), 139, 158; servant of the gods, 162; and his brothers, story of, 162
Agni Jātavedas ("Omniscient"), 164, 189
Ahalyā, story of, 229
Aham brahma asmi, "I am the Brahma," 275
Ahura Mazda (O r m a z d), 120 *ff.,* 126, 133, 232. *See* Asura
Airyama, 129. *See* Aryaman
Ajātaçatru, 219, 227
Akbar, Emperor, 52 *ff.*

À Kempis, Thomas, 281
Alexander the Great, 18, 282
Altar, three altars, 161
Amesha Spentas, "Holy Immortals," 133 *ff.*
Ança, 130
Andra, 176. *See* Indra
Angiras, semi-divine priests, 144, 163
Anquetil du Perron, 54
Antiope of Bœotia, mother of Dioscuri, 116
Āprī–hymns, 78, 79
Apsaras (nymphs), 46, 191
Āranyaka Texts, 49, 50, 209
Arāti, "Demon of Grudge," 191
Arrested anthropomorphism, 85, 93, 165
Arta. See Ṛta
Ārtabhāga, a theosopher, 260
Aryaman, 129, 134, 153
Aryan. *See* Indo-Iranian
Aryans, Indian, geographical provenience of, 23
Ārya Samāj, a reform association, 9
Asceticism, criticised by Buddha, 282; by Professor Huxley, 283
Ascetic wanderer, 288
Asha. See Ṛta
Asura = Ahura, 133
Atharvāngirasah, "blessings and curses," 26, 29
Atharva-Veda, 17, 25 *ff.,* 39, 40 *ff.,* 77; its theosophy, 209

Index

293

Children of "Father Sky," 110, 112
Climate and nature, influence of upon mythology, 82; cause of pessimism, 265
Comparative Mythology, 108, 167; criticism of, 100 ff.
Conflicting prayers and sacrifices, 185
"Cosmic order." *See* Ṛta
Counsel of perfection, 126
Creation hymn, 229, 234 ff.
Creative fervor, 237
Çrotriyas, or "Oral Traditionalists," 21
Çvetaketu Āruni, 223
Çvetāçvatara Upanishad, 279
Cyavana the Bhārgava, story of, 46

D

D a k s h a, a god, 130
Dakshinā, "Baksheesh," name of Ushas, Dawn, 71. *See* Baksheesh
Dāna-stuti, "gift-praises," 196
Dārā Shukoh, a Mogul prince, 52 ff.
Darius I. Hystaspes, 14
Dawn, mother of Agni, 160. *See* Ushas
Death, early notions of, 249 ff.
"Death anew," or "Redeath," 253
D e i v ō s, "Shiners," Indo-European word for gods, 108, 148
"Desire," Kāma, personified, 237
Deucalion, myth of, 138
Deussen, Paul, Professor, 56, 233, 234
Devotion, 195, 202 ff., 281; personified, 206, 273; contrasted with Faith, 193. *Cf.* Prayer.

Devotional (creative) fervor, 237
Dhātar, "Maker," 242
Dhenā, "Holy Song," wife of Brihaspati, 244
Diespiter, Jupiter, 110
Dioscuri. *See* Açvins
Dīrghatamas, author of a riddle-hymn, 210, 217, 229, 233
Djemshed (Yima Khshaeta), Persian epic hero, 143
Dogs of Yama, dogs of death, 105, 106, 251
Dreams and hallucinations, 255
Dyaus, Dyaush Pitar, "Father Sky," 66, 92, 95, 110, 139, 148, 152 ff.

E

Economic conditions and pessimism, 264
Emerson's poem on Brahma, 278
Eros, "Love," personified, 237, 245
Ethics, Vedic system of, 126 ff.
Ethnology, its relation to Mythology, 93

F

Faith, conception of, 109, 186 ff.; personified, 189; faith and works, 190, 269; related to truth and wisdom, 188; reward of, postponed to heaven, 193
"Family-books" of Rig-Veda 27, 79, 210
Father God, 138
Fathers in heaven, 250, 251, 287
"Father Sky." *See* Dyaus.

Metempsychosis. *See* Transmigration
Metres, 24; belonging to
different hours of the day,
80; to individual gods, 80
Mithraism, 85
Mitra (Persian Mithra, Mi-
thras), 92, 120 *ff.*, 129,
132 *ff.*, 153, 210, 218
Moderation in asceticism,
282, 284
Mohammedanism in India,
10, 52 *ff.*
Mokshamūlara, S a n s k r i t
name of Max Müller, 53
Monism, idea of unity, 56 *ff.*,
210, 218, 233, 247, 269.
See Pantheism
Moon and "Sun-Maiden,"
marriage of, 114
Morning and evening star,
114 *ff.*, 172
"Mother Earth," 95, 110,
138, 148
Mountains as winged birds,
legend of, 48
Muir, Dr. John, 154
Müller, Max, 53, 71, 102,
164, 199
Mystics, Christian, 275, 281
Mythology, 29; in its relation
to Ethnology, 103. *Cf.*
Indo-Iranian, and Indo-
European

N

Naciketas, a theosopher, 192,
223
Na neti, "no, no," 277
Nature myth, 29, 81, 108,
148, 152 *ff.*; nature phenomena in legends, 48; in
riddles, 217
Neoplatonism, 207
Nidhanas of the Sāma-Veda,
37

O

Odhin, a Norse god, 155
Oldenberg, H., Professor, 72,
133 *ff.*, 273
Onesikritos, a Greek, 283
Opaque gods, 96, 174
Oupnekhat, Persian trans-
lation of the Upanishads,
54 *ff.*

P

Pairs of gods, 78
Pantheism, 242. *See* Mon-
ism
Pantheon of the Veda, 78,
88 *ff.*
Parāçara, a Rishi, 225
Paradise, 250, 287; solar,
169 *ff.*
Parameshthin, "He who oc-
cupies the highest place,"
242
Parjanya, God of Thunder,
92, 111, 178, 181
"Parliament of Religions,"
in Chicago, 9
Parsis in India, 10, 14, 118
Patrons of sacrifice, 193 *ff.*,
215; of theosophy, 219
Perkunas, Lithuanian God of
Thunder, 111, 115
Persian and Hindu religion
contrasted, 118
Persian names in *arta*, 12
Pessimism, 3, 4, 212, 263;
its origin, 264; its final
fixation, 267
Philosophy, its relation to
practical life, 10. *See* The-
osophy
Phœbus Apollo and Marsyas,
84
Pischel, R., Professor, 113
Poetic inspiration, 75, 201 *ff.*
Popular religion, 42, 77